*W. G. GRACE*

# W. G. GRACE

*His Life and Times*

by ERIC MIDWINTER

London
GEORGE ALLEN & UNWIN
Boston          Sydney

First published in 1981

GEORGE ALLEN & UNWIN LTD
40 Museum Street, London WC1A 1LU


©Eric Midwinter, 1981


British Library Cataloguing in Publication Data

Midwinter, Eric
　W. G. Grace
　1. Grace, William Gilbert
　2. Cricket players – England – Biography
　796.358'092'4　　　GV915.G7


ISBN 0-04-796054-X

Typeset in 11 on 13 point Garamond by Red Lion Setters, London
and printed in Great Britain
by Mackays of Chatham

## DEDICATION

*For John Rennie, Brian Walsh, John Raynor and
other nostalgic and talkative watchers*

# Contents

# List of Illustrations

---

## Cartoon in Text

Punch, September 19, 1885—The End of the Cricketing Season: A few of the Gentlemen Players caught by our artist at Lord's (by Harry Furniss) *page 90*

---

## Acknowledgements

Acknowledgements and thanks are due to the Marylebone Cricket Club for all the illustrations used in this book except for no. 6 (The Beldam Collection), no. 9 and the cartoon in the text (*Punch*) and no. 10 (National Portrait Gallery)

INTRODUCTION

# W. G. GRACE—
# *Most Eminent Victorian*

W. G. Grace is now possibly the most recognisable Victorian per-
sonage, perhaps more easily identified by many people today than the
Queen herself. His career spans the upsurge, climax and decline of the
greatness of Victorian Britain; cricket, with its profound social and
cultural ramifications, formed an integral part of that society, and
Grace was an integral part of cricket.

The emergence of the game of cricket in a shape recognisable to
modern eyes occurred around 1830 to 1835. Three stumps, an end to
charging, a leg before wicket rule, regulations about bat width and
new balls, the treatment of the wicket and the paraphernalia of scores
and averages were, by then, firmly established; and cricket was being
played in thirty-seven English counties, together with a scattering of
Scottish, Welsh and Irish shires. In 1835, the year of the Municipal
Incorporations Act, intended for the saner management of English
boroughs, there was a major overhaul also of the laws of cricket.
These laws were almost universally accepted and are not dissimilar, in
wording and intent, from those of today. It was, we should recall, a
commercial age and one that preferred to keep its ledgers straight.
Racing and boxing, as well as cricket, were also to be subject to that
rational approach, with the consequent demise of many localised or
isolated arrangements.

In cricket, the most obvious change by 1835 from the beginning of
the century was that round-arm bowling replaced under-arm bowling
almost totally, and, in less than thirty years, the final mighty change—
to the over-arm bowling with which we are so familiar—had taken
place and was legally sanctioned. It is also interesting to note the sheer
abundance of cricket matches, while the coverage afforded to them by
the press suddenly swelled in spectacular fashion. In the couple

of decades after 1835, the number of reported games increased four-fold.

1835, or thereabouts, was, therefore, a date of much importance for cricket. And it is more than coincidence that historians also admit 1830 as some kind of social and economic watershed for the country.

Put briefly, demographic, industrial, political and administrative revolutions meshed to create the Victorian state which had its cultural dimension too. Its dour religiosity, its harsh manners, its stern adherence to the work ethic and, above all, its bounding self-assurance and complacency had already settled into a discernible shape by the accession of Queen Victoria in 1837, and it was not to be fundamentally disturbed until the Edwardian decade and the trauma of World War I. More than most reigns, then, Victoria's was a definable phase in the nation's history.

The case of cricket in the Victorian age became particularly clear-cut because it had the equivalent of what Thomas Carlyle labelled in political history its 'great man'. W. G. Grace was born in 1848, soon after the dawn of the Victorian age of cricket; he picked up the game of underhand lobs in country fields, shook it fiercely in both technical and social terms, and handed it, sculpted and honed to its own highest levels of aspiration, to a twentieth century which has, rightly or wrongly, never had the temerity to alter it in any basic manner. Grace was the complete Victorian. Accomplished, egocentric, bumptiously confident, maddeningly fit and untiring, boyishly high-spirited and, by that token, deceitful, extremely money-minded, and, for good and ill, paternalistic. Maybe it is the other way round; maybe it is *because* of W. G. Grace and a few others of the same ilk we conceive thus of the Victorian male.

Florence Nightingale, Cardinal Manning, Thomas Arnold and General Gordon were the subjects of Lytton Strachey's *Eminent Victorians*; but W. G. Grace was certainly a more complete and characteristic Victorian than any of them, for he added to the dedicated fanaticism of Gordon or Nightingale, the vaunting avarice of George Hudson, the Railway King. W. G. Grace, some claim, made more money in real terms than any cricketer up to the present time.

It is the single-mindedness, the zealous devotion to their chosen duty which is so remarkable about the leading Victorians, Grace included. The stamina with which they sustained their command of their selected fields is, on examination, daunting. What flesh allowed, what spirit forced, W. G. Grace to play and practise cricket year after year, in the face of the harsh vicissitudes of travel, catering, accommodation, medical science, and even clothing, at that time?

It is perhaps a trivial illustration but, just as Florence Nightingale engaged herself at Scutari in full Victorian costume so did W. G. Grace face Gregory and Spofforth in unbearable heat—clad for the English spring.

There is another more important quality about the Victorians' obsessiveness. Their commitment was often total enough to make them lop-sided and over-specialised as human beings. One thinks of Gladstone (it was Ronald Knox who plausibly claimed that Grace and the Grand Old Man were one and the same) with his massive reading programmes and his godlike embrace of theology and high finance. In *A Study in Scarlet*, his first Sherlock Holmes story, Conan Doyle makes Dr Watson list his criminologist friend's strengths and weaknesses: strong on the violin, boxing, swordsmanship and, in an 'unsystematic way' anatomy, and 'profound' in chemistry; frail— 'nil' is the word used—in literature, philosophy, politics and, save for poisons, botany. Grace himself was interested in athletics, bowls, and, of course, retained a competent interest in general medical practice. But cricket was his singular objective.

All this helps explain the perspectives of Victorian cricket, perspectives which the present age has not radically redefined. The total commitment of the combatants helped to create a special significance for cricket at county and international level, for cricket adopted political, diplomatic and even military overtones. Such competitiveness in sport, especially in national arenas, was unheard of before Victorian times. Many would say it is worse today, but what is difficult to deny is that the Victorians invented the analogy of the game with the battle, and that some at least of this stemmed from their absolute commitment. For Grace, ranged against the infidel ranks of Australia, Lord's was his Khartoum. While Gladstone was making himself 'the centre of immense popular enthusiasm' in politics, Grace was busily popularising sport. He was the most popular sportsman of the Victorian age, not only in England but throughout the English-speaking world. Because of this, and the related fact that the twin developments of industrial urbanism and spectator sports grew hand in hand, he was, then, the most celebrated sportsman in the entire world. Not until the arrival of Pele or Ali do we find the modern equivalent of the adulation paid Grace.

Oddly, however, he was a man drawn from outside the chief tributaries to the game's mainstream. In Victorian cricket there was distinct and rigid social divorcement of amateur and professional, and yet somehow Grace fitted neither compartment. Which was Grace? Ostensibly he was, of course, the amateur, but he was not the amateur archetype. Most notable amateurs of that age were recruited from the major public schools or the ancient universities, and usually both. Grace, as a youth, knew neither the cricket pitches of Harrow nor those of the Parks. Also he was very highly paid for playing cricket. Probably some of the varsity amateurs were not as pure as their image suggests, but no English amateur has pursued payment so assiduously as W. G. Grace, although it is fair to say that those golden boys normally possessed unearned income.

Grace was a happy mongrel. Not for him the sleek, high-born pedigree of the 'gentleman' nor the tenacious gun-dog application of the 'player'. To call him a 'shamateur' would be misleading, however, for there was little of the conspiratorial about it. He was simply a contradiction: an exceedingly well-paid amateur cricketer, probably earning in some years of his prime the 'real value' equivalent of thousands of pounds by today's reckoning. Wisden of 1897 accepted that 'nice customs curtsey to great kings and the work he has done in perpetuating cricket outweighs a hundredfold every other consideration'.

Naturally, it was his genius which allowed him to ride rough-shod over the establishment, but was it the originality of his social place in that situation which released his genius? His talents were comprehensive: he worked hard to master all approaches to batting rather than, as was the norm, to concentrate on one mode, such as backplay. It is also easily forgotten that he was a prime all-rounder, and one of the few world-class amateur bowlers of the century. Perhaps his was the revolution of the rootless, a refusal to conform because he was not the child of that conformity.

Again one might seek out analogues. Benjamin Disraeli, Jewish, cool, even cynical, a hint of Regency about his debonair, unruffled demeanour, became the general who remarshalled the Conservative Party to fight on the new battle-grounds. Arthur Sullivan, born the son of a clarionetist and of decidedly lower-middle-class origins, became an adored socialite as well as the man who saved the English-speaking musical theatre from the abyss. Both had their counterparts. Gladstone was busily redefining British radical politics, as Disraeli regrouped its conservative elements, and W. S. Gilbert, both as librettist and producer, was, of course, the acidic stimulant for Sullivan's endeavours.

Grace, however, required no competitor nor complement to perform at the most titanic levels and be judged accordingly: batsman and bowler; captain, selector and manager; bearing forward the past and looking to the future. Indeed it is not often, in any walk of life and over such a sustained period that one man has so dominated it. He was both Gladstone and Disraeli to cricket, and he played Sullivan to his own Gilbert.

From a more ordinary viewpoint than that of Grace, one other man illustrates the major themes of Victorian cricket: the professionalism, the colonial aspect, and the county structure. The life and career of William Midwinter throw his master's achievements into starker relief. He is reputed to have been my grandfather's cousin, but more than family respect excuses his presence here. He was the only man to play for England versus Australia and vice versa. His career was entwined with that of Grace, and, in his financial opportunism and cocking of snooks, he reflected, in subdued hues, some of the flamboyance of Grace's character. He also scored the first double century and was the first to carry his bat in Australian cricket; played against England in the first-ever so-called Test match; became, on Grace's proposition, Gloucestershire's first-ever regular professional; was cricket's first transoceanic commuter; and was the first Test cricketer to die.

In the summer of 1979 I made a pilgrimage to St Briavels, the Forest of Dean village where William Midwinter was born. With aid from the vicarage—and having happily noted that my ancestor's name is included in the pamphlet on the church's history—my family and I tracked down the house, a mile or so out of the village and down a terrifyingly steep lane, where he was born. We also met a hospitable and charming man whose uncle had played with the Graces for Gloucestershire. The uncle had had his own Grace story. It concerned W.G.'s brother, E. M. Grace, and the death of his third—out of four—wife, whom he had disliked intensely. Meeting up with him for a cricket match practically on the day of the funeral, the uncle had felt he should say he was sorry. 'H'm', said 'The Coroner' shortly, 'are you? Well, I'm not.' It was among such characters that Billy Midwinter played his cricket.

Dr W. G. Grace was, as for hundreds of others, Midwinter's guide and exemplar: a great man reigning over the most exquisitely harmonious of sports, the one most loved in Victorian England, and that at a time when this nation was at its proudest.

# 1

# Grace's Early Years and the Emergence of Cricket (1848-57)

William Gilbert Grace was born on 18 July 1848, in the busy middle of a cricket season, and with political revolution afoot in many parts of Europe. Mazzini's 'Young Italy' movement was flourishing in Italy and Louis Philippe of France had just abdicated and the Second Republic been declared. A month or so before Grace's birth, the Chartists assembled on Kennington Common (not many yards from the site of some of W.G.'s most splendid exploits at the Oval) prior to presenting their third and final petition to Parliament. It was a year of revolution for cricket as well, for it fell to W. G. Grace to lead cricket to its maturity in terms of skills and of social impact.

He was brought up in a family devoted to the game. Henry Mills Grace, his father, was born in February 1808 and William Gilbert himself died in 1915. Their two lives thus spanned the nineteenth century and its Edwardian postscript, an epoch when, militarily, commercially, technically and internationally, Great Britain enjoyed her historic period of supremacy. And it was by no means coincidental that cricket, most characteristic of English pastimes, came to fruition during this period.

Henry Grace was a Somerset man and came from solid county stock. His background was rural middle class and, by the 1820s, he was an enthusiastic participant in the leisure activities of that class. As a medical student he was eager to rise at five in the morning to practise his cricket with a handful of fellow-zealots on Durdham Downs, and, despite his medical duties, he was frequently to find time to ride with the Duke of Beaufort's hounds. That in itself is an interesting juxtaposition of pursuits, for their lines of development were more or less crossing at that stage. Hunting, for some centuries geared to military training and the province of the well-to-do, was fast becoming more of a diversion with social trappings, while cricket, the one-time sport of children and menials, had been lionised by the aristocracy and was soon to become part of the preparation for life of better-off Victorian youths.

Henry Grace was born and brought up in Long Ashton, a Somerset village hard by the Gloucestershire boundary. It is a wry thought that, had he remained there, his famous son might have played for the 'dragon' county and Somerset might not have waited until 1979 for its first major title. As it was, he completed his medical studies, married and moved into Gloucestershire. It was a journey of no more than five or six miles which took him to Downend, a small village but close enough to Bristol—some four miles—to be regarded as all but a suburb of that city.

He married Martha Pocock in 1831. It was not a propitious time for country folk. The frightening 'Swing' riots of agricultural labourers were taking place in the very counties which nurtured cricket. The rural poor, especially after the disastrous harvest of 1829, were desperate and William Cobbett raged at the discovery of bodies behind hedges, with only 'sour sorrel' in their bellies. In the winter previous to Henry Grace's wedding, arson, minor riots, machine-breaking and other destructive responses of men moved by starvation beyond endurance had occurred in Gloucestershire, and the upshot was a couple of dozen gaol sentences for rioters in the county and as many more shipped to Van Diemen's Land, Tasmania. These were anxious times for the young professional couple: it is as well to remember that the mellow rusticity of the village green with its rough-hewn cricket was but one side of their rural life.

Henry could not, however, have selected a more appropriate consort for his self-appointed task as progenitor of Gloucestershire cricket. Martha became cricket's first lady, indeed, the only female to find her birth and death recorded in the male chauvinist pages of *Wisden*.

Her father, George Pocock, was an eccentric schoolmaster, at St Michael's Hill, Bristol, in the grand Regency tradition. His twin obsessions—box-kites and evangelical religion—were dissimilar except in intensity. Like the barn-storming preachers of Wild West lore, he travelled around erecting a tent to attract sinners in spots too wild for conventional church development. His 'itinerant temple', as he called it, was almost as famous locally as his powerful box-kites.

These actually drew coaches, and once George Pocock tangled with a
high-born nobleman and his horse-drawn carriage over a serious over-
taking issue.

The redoubtable Martha was his intrepid passenger in a chair flight,
powered by box-kite, across the Avon Gorge, and a gusty change of
wind that day might well have altered the course of cricket's saga. Her
brother, a joint survivor of this bizarre upbringing, was also to play an
important part in the early years of the Grace story. This was W. G.
Grace's uncle Alfred, and, during their youth, he was to act as cricket
instructor to the Grace boys. Day after day he was to march the twelve
mile round trip from his own home to the Grace residence and back in
order to supervise their practice sessions. There can have been few
more successful coaches. Apart from his influence on W.G., Alfred
Pocock, no mean club cricketer himself, helped train all the Graces.
They were to become the core of a championship-winning county side.

As was usual in those times, the families were well-matched
socially. The Pococks were well-to-do gentry, with much the same
four-square values as the Graces. They were both respectable, conservative, dedicated and authoritarian families, ready to work, play and
undertake civic duties. But Henry and Martha were to become an
atypical nineteenth-century couple. They put behind them the wilder
enthusiasms of Martha's father and committed themselves to a sober
but no less exacting life, packed with strenuous activity. They inherited George Pocock's energy, but not his oddity. Henry Grace would
ride, his son was later to explain, six miles to the east at dawn to visit a
patient, and then, after his usual rounds, he would ride six miles to the
west at midnight to assist another patient—and still find time for
cricket practice. The social status to which Grace was born was to
prove important on two counts. In the most literal sense, it was middle
class and, automatically, it thrust W. G. Grace between the two
classes, upper and lower, from which most notable cricketers had and
were to come. Beyond this, it placed him in that social category which,
with an admixture of economic, religious and social beliefs, was
presently making a deity of the work ethic and creating a life-style
around it.

Mrs Grace was born on 18 July 1812. She was thus scarcely nineteen on her wedding day, and when, in 1850, she had assembled a
family of nine, five boys and four girls, she was still under forty; but,
again in character with the age, the emphasis was firmly placed on the
boys, and, except as occasional fielders and marriage fodder, the
daughters were to have no part in the unfolding narrative.

Of the four boys, the first, taking as was normal the paternal fore-name, was Henry, born in 1833. After a seven-year break, the next two sons arrived close together: Alfred in 1840 and Edward in 1841. There was another dearth of males for a further seven years, before William Gilbert, on his mother's own birthday, in 1848, and then Fred, in 1850, were born. There was thus a seventeen-year gap between the eldest and youngest of the Graces, so that by the time they were all competing equally as grown men Henry was approaching forty.

This also meant that, before W. G. Grace's birth, let alone boyhood, the cricketing stage was being set. In 1845, when Henry junior was twelve and ready to be blooded in useful company, Henry senior established Mangotsfield Cricket Club. Mangotsfield was the parent parish of Downend, where the Graces lived, and it covered a sizeable area. From this neighbourhood Henry Grace had to recruit not only players, but a labour force to clear the gorse and bracken of Rodway Hill Common not far from Mangotsfield Station.

Strangely, it was in that same year, 1845, that cricket, along with other ball games, was legalised, although, of course, the ancient laws forbidding such sports had long gone unenforced. This was because the higher social orders had taken over their servants' unlawful diversions, and nothing is more ironic for the sport 'least spoilt by any form of vice' than that its London-based consolidation was based on that most debilitating of sins, gambling. Indeed (as with racing and boxing, then cricket's counterparts) the need to observe laws or 'articles of agreement' and to study 'form' was in large part a consequence of the gambling fever. Hitherto, cricket, along with a score of other ball-and-target diversions, had probably been much more localised and variable than the antiquarians, determined to find what Christopher Brookes terms 'a respectable pedigree' for their favoured sport, might have hoped. Rather was there a concept of 'gameness', of a thousand and one alternatives each played by autonomous groups parochially.

Cricket, then, emerged slowly from that variety of sporting life, first to adopt its own peculiar configuration and next to shake off its disreputable gambling image. Here was Henry Mills Grace, categorically middle class, along with hundreds of other doctors, schoolmasters, parsons and farmers, offering some synthesis to a game which, socially speaking, had developed on either side of him. That this harmony, this sense of a sport technically regulated and socially accepted, had been achieved by the accession of Victoria meant that the stage was properly set for W. G. Grace.

By the end of Henry Grace's boyhood cricket had also become a predominantly English game. After the American War of Independence, cricket tended to atrophy across the Atlantic, despite some manful perseverance, especially in the vicinity of Philadelphia. Equally, the French Wars amputated continental cricket (particularly promising in the Channel Ports) from the body of cricket proper. The 1783-1815 period ensured that England was almost exclusively the haven of cricket at that very juncture when it reached fulfilment, and, apart from the effects in the Americas and in Europe, such isolation meant that there may have been reverse losses of influence on the English game from both these sources.

So, just as men like Henry Grace were pulling together the threads of cricket's development into a discernible, countrywide pattern, there was this temporary end to ramifications overseas. As the game flourished internally, it withered abroad. Henry Grace was presenting his sons with a mature and well-seasoned recreation, but one peculiarly English. Other families—the Brenchleys of Gravesend and the Bakers of Canterbury—were as active. But only the Graces of Downend produced a nonpareil.

Idyllically rural though the village of Downend may have been, it stood on the outskirts of Bristol which, until the onset of the Industrial Revolution, had long been England's second city and was to maintain much of its wealth and pre-eminence thereafter. In 1851 its population was 166,000 (when London's was two million) and it had doubled in size since Henry Grace's birth. The lives of the Graces were not becalmed in rustic backwaters, and the import of urban settlement on first-class cricket was to be confirmed by the part played by Bristol. There is a running element of the golden mean throughout W. G. Grace's career. Born to a midway place between upper and lower orders, he was bred in rural environs with strong urban overtones. Cricket was, in its infancy, a rural sport, but it was weaned by the towns. Just as he was well placed socially to interpret cricket's sociological balance, Grace was admirably located geographically to benefit from its ecological harmony.

Nobody could have commenced a sporting career earlier. He claimed that he handled a bat at the age of two. That was the year— 1850—when the family moved from Downend House to 'Chestnuts', some small distance away, and it was there that they constructed their world-famous practice pitch. Trees in the eighty-yard orchard to the left of the house were felled and the soil cleared and flattened. That corner of reclaimed land was to suffer the hardest of poundings. Year after year, day by day, the Graces practised unrelentingly. They began in early March to be well rehearsed for the coming season; they persevered as late as October, practising when the season itself had more or less closed. They rose early to get best use of the light, and they trained assiduously in the evenings, often under the omniscient eye of Uncle Alfred.

As soon as Gilbert was at all mobile, he joined the fray, with one brother, Henry, now twenty, and Alfred and Edward in their early teens. The dogs—Ponto, Dan and Noble—fielded with skill and devotion, scurrying, collecting and returning for as long as the family had the stamina to bat and bowl. Grace's biographers, not least A. A. Thomson, have rejoiced particularly in Ponto. It is recorded that, a lifelong purist, he sat quite tightly, barked angrily and refused to field when E. M. Grace indulged his ugly but highly effective cross-bat swat. The rulings were few and simple. The grown-ups batted for fifteen minutes and the youngsters for five minutes, giving a norm over the years of two to three hours a session. Apparently dissatisfied with the adult-child differential, Gilbert and his younger brother Fred used to recruit, in typically middle-class style, the boot-boy and Tibbie Jones, the nursemaid, as slave labour for even more practice. Sadly, the girls were classified with the dogs: they sometimes were allowed—indeed, required—to field, but they were not permitted to bat. Eternal substitutes, they existed to service the endeavours of the young males.

By good fortune all the boys (whether all the girls is not reported) entered into the spirit of this saturation training without cavil or complaint. All became noted cricketers and only Alfred, the comparative failure, did not make a notable contribution to cricket's history, but he had, and not just metaphorically, the last laugh, outliving them all by date and years, dying in 1916, aged seventy-six. That they appeared to enjoy it sometimes distracts attention from the overall intensity of the indoctrination.

It was not out of keeping with current views on education. In the wake of John Locke, Benthamites such as James Mill were keen to view the child's mind and body as a *tabula rasa*, whereon whatever the mentor chose could be written. For the Victorians, the child was father to the man. Hence the concept of the 'little man' or 'little woman' evidenced in Victorian fashion, where children are invariably dressed in adult clothing, or in the elaborate mature thoughts placed in children's minds by contemporary novelists. W.G. was later to say that he was not born a cricketer, but that he was 'born in the atmosphere of cricket'.

This, together with the Victorian trust in hard labour, probably informed the Downend experiment in concentrated instruction. 'I had to work as hard at cricket', said W.G. in later years, 'as ever I worked at my profession or anything else.' It was not so far removed from Mr Gradgrind and Mr Bounderby in Dickens's *Hard Times* (published in 1854) with their credo of force-feeding 'facts'. When he was six, and as part of this drilling, Gilbert, as he was then known in his domestic circle, was taken in the dog cart by his mother, the brisk, short ride into Bristol. It was 1854, with the Crimean War about to unleash its nastiness on Britain's soldiers, and the occasion was a match between the All-England XI and XXII from the Bristol area. This West Gloucestershire team was captained by Henry Mills Grace, and he was supported by his son, Henry, and his brother-in-law, Alfred Pocock.

The All-England XI initiated one of the most fascinating phases in the development of professional cricket, and it was one in which Grace was to be substantially involved. Cricket provided an uncommon illustration of an integrated culture, with master and man well met on equal terms. Although comparable to racing and boxing, which also had true-blue patrons and popular heroes, cricket was the team game *par excellence*, and the one in which master and servant joined forces. Cricket's great virtue of encouraging contest without physical contact was the social characteristic which enabled master to play with and against servants. From this phenomenon grew the strict class division of amateur and professional but, during Gilbert's childhood and after- wards, the professional was in the ascendant. William Clarke, the one- eyed under-arm bowler from Nottingham, was the key figure, as, six days a week, five months a year, his All-England XI played over thirty matches a season, normally against odds. These tireless cricketers carried top-class cricket, missionary-style, to the most outlandish parts of the kingdom, and, such was their dominance, the Gentlemen won only seven of their fixtures with the Players in the first twenty- eight years of Victoria's reign.

Occasionally Gentlemen did play for Clarke's troupe, acting in part as its social frontmen, so much so that there was obviously already a twilight zone between complete amateur and full-time professional, which W. G. Grace, especially when running the United South of England XI, one of seven such cadres to be so established, was later to enjoy with relish. The exhibition XIs were not profit-sharing (not with William Clarke at the helm, who may well have profited by over a thousand pounds a season) but there was a whiff of syndicalism about them in those years when the Equitable Pioneers were beginning cooperative trading in Rochdale. The Clarkes and Wisdens and Lilly-whites were more perhaps the equivalents of the inventor-craftsmen of the Industrial Revolution, men like Richard Arkwright, James Brindley and George Stephenson. But, most of all, the entrepreneu-rial professionals were entertainers: their contemporaries were the itinerant theatrical companies. Vincent Crummles, Dickens's expan-sive repertory manager, was William Clarke's Thespian alternate, and, indeed, the first part of *Nicholas Nickleby* was published in 1838.

Thus it was that the six-year-old Grace, unconscious of what had led to the arrival of Clarke and his exhibition team in Bristol, watched excitedly from his perch on the family trap. The match took place over two days on a field behind the Full Moon Hotel at Stockes Croft in Bristol. William Caffyn, the Surrey all-rounder, George Parr, 'the Lion of the North', and the nervy, little, oddly named batsman Julius Caesar played alongside William Clarke. Alfred Mynn umpired and 'Old Under-arm', as Clarke was nicknamed, captured eighteen wickets. But young Grace's delight at watching his father, uncle and brothers take on the might of those household names may have been tempered by the crushing nature of Bristol's defeat, which was by a margin of 149 runs. Alfred Pocock and young Henry contributed two of the only four double-figure scores of the forty-four innings. Dr Grace managed but 3 and 0 but his son, Henry, also took three wickets. The engagement was covered by Mr Wintle, the landlord of the Full Moon Hotel, to the tune of £65, and, typically, the England team travelled all night, having finished a match in Leicestershire the previous evening. What the *Bristol Mercury* called 'numbers of jolly citizens' certainly made the most of the occasion, sitting 'under tents Turk-like enjoying their pipes of peace and tankards of home-brewed'.

The fixture was repeated the following summer, and this time the boy's pleasure was intensified. Clarke was taken enough with E. M. Grace's 'extraordinary skill' at longstop to present him with a bat, and, in honour of Mrs Grace's accurate grasp of the game and encouragement of her family, the old cricketer gave her a copy of W. Bolland's *Cricket Notes*, which included 'practical hints' of his own. Those that knew William Clarke, now fifty-seven years of age, doubt-less saw this as a shrewd commercial investment. The match itself was once more a disappointment for the provincials. It was all, as the *Mercury* opined, 'very mortifying', as, led by Julius Caesar's 33 and 78, All-England raced to a 165-run victory. There were twenty ducks in the two Bristol innings, with Henry, his father and his uncle Alfred being the only ones to reach double figures. Going in last, the thirteen-year-old Edward Grace scored I and 3, being, at the first attempt, leg before to a ball from Willsher which struck him in the waistcoat. 'The bat was seldom raised', said the *Bristol Mercury*, 'to give a vigorous blow.'

It is not a question of gloating over the vanquished locals, but of emphasising the paucity of country cricket at that stage. These were the first two representative games to take place in Gloucestershire and the first cricket matches to be reported in the Bristol press—'we are but scantily versed in this fine exercise', its reporter disarmingly confessed. It was the middle of the last century, and Bristol—where within recent years the *Great Western*, one of the first transatlantic steamships, and the *Great Britain*, the first iron ship, had been built—was an important centre. And yet cricket had, at that point and in that locale, scarcely made an impact.

Thus it was back to the Graces' equivalent of the drawing board, to wit the orchard, for practice, and ever more practice. The ignominy of those defeats must have rankled with that proud family. Famed they may have been, but, after all, William Caffyn was a hairdresser by trade and William Clarke had started working life as a bricklayer. Of course, cricket might have dominated day-by-day life, but it could not monopolise it completely. There were other sports, and young Gilbert, like his brothers, became a straight and true shot by the time he was a teenager. Then there was school. Alfred and Edward were educated at Kempe's School, Long Ashton, near Bristol, and before that Edward boarded at Goodenough House in Ealing, a school kept by George Gilbert, Uncle Pocock's brother-in-law. For whatever reason, Henry, Gilbert himself and the younger Fred did not attend either school. It may have been short-term changes in the family finances which enabled sons number two and three, but not one, four and five to enjoy that kind of schooling. It may just have been cricket—Edward had to be specially fetched from Kempe's to make his celebrated appearance against Clarke's team, and the elder Henry was not the man to let education stand in the way of cricket.

Whatever the cause, Gilbert was always available for cricket practice and never travelled far to school. He went as a small child to Miss Trotman's little establishment in the village, which was probably no more than a dame's school or kindergarten. After a spell under the private tutelage of Mr Curtis, a teacher from Winterbourne, he attended Rudgeway House School, another local institution owned by Mr Malpas. A master there, Mr Bernard, was soon to become Gilbert's brother-in-law. He turned his hand to medicine and married Alice Grace. Rumour has it that his courtship was abetted by his pupil, encouraged by gifts of confiscated marbles—an early instance of W.G.'s shrewd opportunism.

Grace stayed at Rudgeway House until he was fourteen, but apart from the indisputable advantage that he was ever-ready for practice and match-play, Gilbert's lack of conventional schooling has another social significance. At that time upper-middle and upper-class families automatically sent their boys to public school, and, almost without exception, the amateur cricketers of Grace's era were former public schoolboys. Again Grace's inter-class status compels attention. His family, through lack of funds, lack of standing, or a refusal to live up to the social norms, did not provide him with this seal of approval; however, had he gone to public school, it is unlikely that Grace would have played as much cricket or of such a competitive brand, but the omission was another element in the curious role, part-amateur, part-professional, he was to play in the game. In so far as he harboured regrets, twinges of rancour may later have affected him as he mixed and played with the Etonians and Harrovians of his day. It is not just that he insisted on his own son going to Clifton, but that his obsession as a selector with public school and university students—one of the chief causes of his eventual break with Gloucestershire in 1899—possibly went beyond the bounds of a purely cricketing judgement.

What is certain is that, aged nine, W. G. Grace made his cricketing debut, and, had he been far away at school, that might well have been postponed. Indeed he was barely nine. The match in question took place on 19 July 1857, a day after his ninth birthday, when W.G. represented West Gloucestershire against Bedminster, one of the stronger XIs in the Bristol area. He contrived to score 3 not out. He batted last and his innings was reported in *Bells' Life* of 26 July. His brother Henry had been fifteen and his brother Edward fourteen before they first played regularly for the club, but Dr Henry Grace was determined to blood his talented infant as quickly as possible. He played two other games that summer, both against Clifton, but managed only a single in three innings. It was a beginning impressive only in so far as this was a child playing with men.

# 2
# Grace's Youth and the Spread of Cricket (1857-66)

The Industrial Revolution is often thought of solely as a northern phenomenon, but Bristol and its surrounds were also vitally affected. It was a case of swings and roundabouts. Gloucestershire's sweepingly open sheep walks were no more. By the time Grace played his first club cricket, the wool industry had deteriorated, with only the Stroudwater area of any import. Here the uneven struggle against the plentiful and cheaper worsted suitings was successfully combatted for a few decades by a concentration on a bizarre pot pourri of specialism, including military scarlets, hunting pinks, green billiard cloths and piano fabric.

In place of wool were the coming enterprises. Coal fed industrialism, and the south-west coal-fields, while small in comparison with their northern counterparts, showed dramatic rises in production. About a million tons of coal were produced each year in the area, and the locations—Mangotsfield, Kingswood, Bedminster, Coalpit Heath—were to keep appearing in local cricket annals, scarcely in keeping with the idyllic notion of pastoral village cricket. As for Bristol, it became the centre for a comprehensive series of secondary industrial products such as watches, soaps, candles, tobacco and chocolate, while milk and cheese became the main farming products of the area.

From a cricketing viewpoint the significant prerequisite of this commercial bustle was transport. Although the trails kept to the high ground, there was no main route for wagons and coaches from Bristol in 1800 which could be guaranteed for all weathers. It was John Macadam who, as surveyor for the Bristol Turnpike Trust, pioneered his celebrated macadamised surfaces in the ten or so years after 1815, and Bristol's outer road network was then one of the city's joys. It was, however, the railways which were to prove most decisive. Mangotsfield Junction, close by the Grace residence, was a stage on the tramway used as a base for the Bristol-Birmingham railway, opened in 1844. Three years earlier, in 1841, the Great Western Railway had linked Bristol with London, via Swindon, Chippenham and Bath. In 1845 the Cheltenham and South-Western Company opened up the Swindon, Stroud, Gloucester and Cheltenham railway, and the whole area was soon a criss-cross of rail communications and competing companies. Macadam roads were followed by Brunel railways. By the time W. G. Grace was poised on the threshold of his national cricketing career, Bristol had developed a communications system the equal of anywhere in the country, which meant, at that time, anywhere in the world.

W. G. Grace, then, grew up as a boy well-versed in rural cunning, but with a railway and a coal mine practically within sight, and with the eastern tracts of Bristol already threatening to embrace his home village. No less a person than Karl Marx has rhapsodised on the perfection of a life-style matching town and country. Certainly W.G. was no stranger to town life, and, although said to be a little ungainly in manner as well as physique as a youth, this was probably no more than the natural gaucheness of adolescence. He was by no means the awed country lad, lost and wondering amid the city lights.

A steady and logical, never brilliant, pupil, W.G. attended Rudgeway House School until he was fourteen, at which point the curate of Downend, the Rev. John Dann, was hired to visit Chestnuts as his tutor. Once more W.G. helped play the unwitting Eros, for the curate married Blanche, another of the Grace daughters. Not that he could have identified the classical allusion. One summery afternoon the Rev. John Dann was wrapped in the study of Horace, specifically the ode that runs 'linked to the nymphs the comely Graces dance along the ground'. The tutor asked for the names of the three Graces. Whether in comic evasiveness or whether awoken from a genuine reverie is not apparent, but young Gilbert, more in the style of *Wisden* than Horace, replied 'E.M., W.G. and G.F.'.

To the horror of his sisters, W.G. was an indefatigable collector of birds' eggs and snakes, and, as in most normal households, debates were joined about where most appropriately such items might be accommodated. Less usually, but in keeping with the rural aspects of his upbringing, he was very early inducted into shooting and following the hounds. There is really no gainsaying the precocity of the child. A mere nine year old, but 'born a big specimen of his race' he had already played club cricket, and was something of a fair shot and huntsman. It is true to say, nonetheless, that his cricket was not successful over its first three years. His four runs in 1857 were followed, in the next two seasons, by a beggarly 16 runs in thirteen knocks.

The West Gloucester club arose from an amalgamation in 1846 of Henry Grace's Mangotsfield outfit with the original West Gloucester club run by a Mr H. Hewitt some four miles away at Coalpit Heath. Quite simply, Henry Grace's team was much superior to the few other XIs in the locality. It was very much, of course, a family affair, with the Graces and Pococks well represented, alongside nephews of Martha Grace, such as William Rees and George Gilbert. The usual composition of other club sides then was a few university students, when they became available during the long vacation, tricked out with a local stalwart or so, and coached by the parson. West Gloucester weighed in a little too heavily for such combines, and it was probably a mix of filial sympathy and overall superiority anyway which permitted them the luxury of including one or more of the Grace children at tender ages.

It was not always a scene of gentle pleasures for these youngsters. In 1858, when the Redland fixture was about to be played on Rodway Hill Common, one belligerent critic protested vociferously at the ground being cleared. These were the days of unenclosed grounds, as 'common' implied, and conscientious objectors, eager to couple the defence of civil liberties with the creation of rowdy nuisance, were not unknown. Alfred Grace violently rejected this socio-political appeal, but, by an hour before close of play, the protestant had recruited a number of well-lubricated companions to assist him. Alfred once more took up the cudgels, and this individual altercation led to a pitched battle, the cricketers taking some early punishment. Both teams rallied, and, shoulder to shoulder, and armed with bats and stumps, they charged the newfound enemy. The struggle lasted for an extraordinary half-hour, until, in fact, Dr Henry Grace returned with a magistrate to read the Riot Act and superintend the dispersal of the intruders. It sounds as if there might have been a little social spikiness to the encounter, with the resentful invaders being of an inferior class—it is unlikely Henry Grace would have turned a JP loose on his social equals. One can imagine that the Graces might have lorded it a little over the common, and, having worked so hard to rid the pitch of gorse and bracken, they might be forgiven. It is possible that an imperious edge to their commands did little to alleviate the bitterness, and, all in all, the anecdote hints at a game very different to the 'country house' exclusiveness which was so much a feature of nineteenth-century cricket.

W. G. Grace, aged ten, was certainly present, if not playing, in the game which led to this fracas, and a strange part of his sporting education it formed. Unluckily, the years of dearth continued for the young fledgling Grace, with one pleasing exception. Over the two days after his twelfth birthday in July 1860, he went in eighth versus Clifton and scored his very first half-century. A good time was had by all his relations. He was preceded by E. M. Grace with 150 and Uncle Pocock with 44 (they amassed 126 for the opening stand). Not out overnight, W.G. completed his own fifty the second morning, and remained undefeated on 51, the innings, it seems, being prolonged for the milestone to be reached. That apart, he managed only 130 runs in his other eighteen innings over the 1860-2 seasons, but W. G. Rees, his cousin and godfather, presented him with a bat for his half-century.

In the meanwhile the other brothers were progressing. Henry was married and settled into his Kingswood Hill medical practice by 1860. Kingswood was a nearby village, with coal mined in its forested fringes, and its mixed populace of farm-hands and colliers were fortunate in their doctor. Henry junior was regarded very highly; his younger brother said of him: 'my brother Henry, he was a *good* doctor, he was', as if the other brothers were less so. Henry remained a keen cricketer, captaining the Hanham side, for whom both Alfred and Gilbert were occasionally to play.

As for that colourful character, E. M. Grace, he was now eighteen or so, and had already become a power in local cricket circles. At sixteen he had played for XXII of Bath versus the United England XI, although, truth to tell, he did not bowl, he was bowled without scoring and succeeded in running out poor old Uncle Pocock for a single. A couple of inches shorter than the Grace average—the father, Henry, Alfred and Fred were about 5 feet 9 or 10 inches, but Edward was barely 5 feet 7 inches—his stocky frame was seen on many, many grounds. At this time he managed to play for Lansdown (near Bath), Clifton, Bedminster, the Medical Men and a few scratch teams as well as West Gloucester, and, aged seventeen, took 173 wickets and scored 1,121 runs. He scored his first century—104 for West Gloucestershire against Bedminster—and the following year he added Berkeley and South Wales to his formidable list of clubs. He was a much travelled

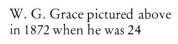

W. G. Grace pictured above
in 1872 when he was 24

W.G., aged 25

A Grace family group taken at Knowle Park, Almondbury, Glos., with Dr H. M. Grace in the top hat in the back row and W.G. on the left of the middle row

Martha Grace, W.G.'s mother

E. M. Grace

G. F. Grace

The Gloucestershire team of 1877 with
W. G. Grace seated holding the bat

W. E. Midwinter who also appears
above, third from right

MIDWINTER

teenager: it was a nine miles walk to Lansdown, for instance, while all the brothers would now occasionally march the four miles to Bristol for coaching with Uncle Pocock. In 1860 E. M. Grace not only played against the All-England XI but for them, against XXII of Devon and Cornwall, at Plymouth, where he scored 24 and 17 not out.

It was Uncle Pocock's view that Edward's cross-bat squat was a consequence of using a full-sized bat when an infant. Time after time, E.M. would drag the ball at right angles from outside the off stump past square leg. Productive it may have been, classical it was not, and Uncle Pocock was not the son, for nothing, of a schoolmaster who had, apart from putting many chimneys at hazard with his kite power, invented a caning machine, the better to persuade his charges to adopt an academic approach. He insisted that W.G. practise and play with a smaller, sawn-down bat adjusted to his size, and many believe that this purposeful attitude—against some opposition, it is said, from his brother-in-law, Grace's father—was a major influence on W.G.'s orthodoxy.

With both W.G. and G.F. showing a talented and keen interest in the game, it was at about this time decided to improve the orchard training ground. E.M. cut turf under the roadside hedges, carted it back home and laid it diligently. Orthodox instruction on tidy pitches began to tell, but not before W.G. endured what proved to be a frightening but beneficial sickness. In the spring of 1863 the fourteen year old contracted a dangerous bout of pneumonia. Anxiously nursed, he was feverish for several weeks and enfeebled for a further period, so much so that it was July and on to his fifteenth birthday before he managed to practise. Nevertheless, in 19 innings he scored 350 runs, far outstripping his total to date. Clifton were the victims of his second half-century. Returning from his sickbed, he scored 82 in his very first match, and later enjoyed an undefeated 52 against Somerset.

Part of this success was a consequence of his abrupt and unprecedented increase in height. Almost as if recovery from pneumonia released some hidden impetus, he rapidly gained several inches, and, within that summer, outgrew father, uncle and brothers. Extra height and power transformed the fourteen-year-old lad into the fifteen-year-old youth. For the first time he was able to overpower Henry, then thirty, in their boisterous horse-play.

His prowess earned him a place, alongside his father, his uncle and his brother, Edward, in the Bristol and Didcot XVIII which once more challenged the professional skills of the All-England XI on Durdham Down. The local newspapers were ecstatic: 'the marvellous agility and vigour displayed will equal, if not surpass, what we read of in the games of ancient Greece and Rome and in the tournaments of the middle ages'.

In actual fact, that journalistic licence was closer to the truth than usual. The All-England XI had a strong side. Stephenson, the Surrey stumper, Caesar, and Willsher, the left-handed pace bowler, made return visits, this time accompanied by the frail but graceful Hayward, uncle of Surrey's Tom Hayward, and those fiercesome bowlers, the dangerous Tarrant and Nottingham's John Jackson. But there were problems. The team was about to embark for Australia, and the arrangements for this, which the players had to resolve themselves, proved too much, especially coming at the end of a typically exhausting summer programme. Bristol removed the All-England XI for 86 and 106. W.G. bowled Stephenson twice, while Edward's success—he took ten wickets in the match—led to them carrying him off to Australia with them, more or less on the spur of the moment. Bristol scored 212, thereby winning by an innings and 20, and W.G. enjoyed a spirited knock of 32.

It was 31 August 1863, and there was W.G. Grace, a month past his fifteenth birthday, playing, and playing well, in his first representative match. 'A lanky, loose-limbed youth' was how the press described him, 'full of life and vim'. His success, coupled with the greater glory enjoyed by Edward, must have delighted the family elders, encouraging them in the belief that the investment was beginning to pay. In a curious postscript, reminiscent of the affray five years earlier on Rodway Hill, the organiser of the Bristol-AEE match, Sykes Bramhall, but using the pseudonym of Captain Rose, was sued for assault. This sporting gentleman was charged with physically molesting a non-cricketer who strenuously resisted being driven from the arena when the game was about to commence. It is strange that, even for so notable a fixture, one had to rely on the goodwill of the citizenry to permit play to begin. Luckily for Captain Rose, the magistrate was a sports-lover, doubtless well pleased at Bristol's triumph over the usually impregnable All-England XI, and the accused was acquitted.

But these excitements were no more than a preface to the stirring deeds of young W.G.'s sixteenth summer, 1864. Topping 6 feet, and with that 'lanky, loose-limbed' frame filling out rapidly, the incessant tuition of a decade began to tell, added, as it now was, to great vigour, a calmness of temperament and the burgeoning of judgement. Although scoring only 15, he was honoured by an invitation to play for the All-England XI, captained by the somewhat neurotic George

Parr, against a Lansdown XVIII, and then came his first match in London. This was something of a breakthrough, and reflected the widening compass of club fixtures at that time. Along with his brother Henry, he journeyed to London for the very first time, a member of the South Wales touring team. His brother, Edward had not returned from Australia in time to join the tour, and the youngster replaced him.

In his first match in London he scored 5 and 38 at the Oval for the South Wales CC against the Surrey club. He was dropped for the other fixture, at the Old Ground, Brighton, in favour of an MCC player, and the family wrath was inflamed. Henry sternly insisted that his young brother had been recruited for both games and that, if one brother did not play, neither should the other. After some bitter debate, the adolescent hopeful looming in the background, the South Welsh skipper capitulated. Young W.G. steeled himself. His place was the result of somewhat crude moral leverage, and humiliation would be the price of failure. The family honour was sustained. The Gentlemen of Sussex were on the receiving end of W.G.'s first-ever century and he followed up his massive 170 with 56 not out. Later that year he twice played at Lord's, and scored a half century against MCC to mark that initial occasion.

It was not all beer and skittles. He managed to negotiate one of his only four recorded pairs of spectacles playing for XXII of Bath versus AEE, at Lansdown. The veteran bowler, Tinley, chastened him both times, but it is salutary to recall that W. G. Grace never suffered the horror of the double duck in first-class cricket. He played for Clifton, as well as West Gloucester, during that summer, and for the first time scored a thousand runs, 400 of them in first-class cricket.

He went better in 1865, scoring 2,169 in all games for an average of 40, with 300 of these runs coming in 13 first-class matches. He made his debut for the Gentlemen at Lord's, and also played in the Oval match. Significantly, the Gentlemen defeated the Players at Lord's after losing nineteen matches consecutively, and Grace was, of course, to exert an enormous and, from the Players' viewpoint, baleful effect on that fixture for many years. He scored only 23 and 12, but took seven for 125 on his first appearance for the Gentlemen, and took thirteen wickets for the Gentlemen of the South versus the Players of the South. Together with his brothers Henry and Edward, he helped a Lansdown XVIII bring the All-England XI to yet another of their rare defeats: they collapsed, 99 and 87, in the two innings. G. F. 'Fred' Grace, the youngest and perhaps most graceful of the brothers, was now fifteen and he, too, was pushing to the fore.

Sceptics might have spoken dismissively of flashes in the pan but 1866 silenced the scoffers. At the end of July, a bare fortnight after his eighteenth birthday, he assembled his first major top-class century, and, as if to emphasise the point, he carried his bat for 224 out of 521 for All-England at the Oval against Surrey. That was the game made almost as celebrated by the decision of V. E. Walker, the England captain, to grant leave to W.G. on the second day to compete in the quarter-mile hurdles at the National Olympian Association Meeting at the Crystal Palace. He jumped the twenty hurdles in the brisk time of a minute and ten seconds, and few England captains have since been so tolerant as Walker. The Oval was one of Grace's favourite grounds. He scored 173 and took nine wickets for the Southern Gentlemen versus the Southern Players and captured another seven wickets in the Oval Gentlemen versus Players fixture that year. The Surrey club presented him with a bat for these exploits.

He bludgeoned three more centuries in club cricket; and made his first visit north, leading XVIII Colts of Nottingham and Sheffield against the All-England XI, and, all in all, totalled close on 3,000 runs, 640 of them in first-class fixtures, at an average of 51. That apart, his slinging, eager round-arm bowling brought him dozens of wickets, and it was reported that 'his fielding at long leg was magnificent'.

Thus in that sharp, whirling flurry of adolescent energy, W. G. Grace had altered the game's frame of reference. That youthful burst of high attainment began to change men's notions of what was possible in cricket. An average of 50 or 60 was uncommon; one of 20 or so was more usual, while his 224 at the Oval was far and away the tallest score recorded there. It must be stressed that wickets were poor to the point of grave danger, and fast bowlers plentiful enough. Grace himself said of this time that 'batsmen were constantly damaged' on 'positively dangerous wickets' and that 'it was no unusual thing to have two or three shooters an over'. With so many playing areas common land, unprotected from a rough-shod public and with, as an additional hazard, creases cut an inch deep in the turf, risks were ever present. George Summers, the young Nottinghamshire professional, had been killed at Lord's by a fast ball from Platts, opening the bowling for the MCC. Richard Daft has recorded his emotions at having to face the next one. That famous and redoubtable bruiser, Jem Mace, told Pooley, the Surrey wicket-keeper, that he would prefer an hour in the ring to five minutes behind the stumps. The young W. G. Grace's rigorous straightness, brute power and remarkable eye not only saved him but enabled him to attack. He was beginning his task of shaping a game.

Of course his actions were not as conscious as that. Like the rest of his family, he was, above all, desperately keen to play cricket with consistent success. What is important is that his achievements occurred as the rollicking expansiveness of the eighteenth century gave way to the sober moralities of the nineteenth. It was, ostensibly, a more religious age, one as much impressed by good works as by passive virtue.

Somehow cricket managed to change its image accordingly. Where in the eighteenth century it had been branded by the more godly and civic-minded as 'not only improper but mischievous', in the nineteenth it came to be regarded as beyond reproach. The cricketer, once little above the apes, was now closer than men to the angels. Somewhat naively, the new Victorian Christians sought in cricket and other sports a manly substitute for the lusts of the flesh. It was the era of 'Muscular Christianity' and a preoccupation with physical fitness. In the early years of the Victorian age, Thomas Arnold of Rugby and Edward Thring of Uppingham had exerted much influence on the public schools and, subsequently, the universities. Thring looked broadly at the quality to be found in people. His biographer termed this the notion of the 'good fellow' which included 'the fool in form' who 'made good hits to the leg'.

Soon the public schools were to be criticised for an over-emphasis on games and athleticism, and it is true that Rugby's 'godliness' became Eton's 'manliness' in the last quarter of the century. Between 1860 and 1880 games became 'compulsory, organised and eulogised' at most public schools; in particular, Eton made games the 'infallible prescription'. Only through games could 'fortitude, self-rule, public spirit—measure in victory, firmness in defeat', be taught. *Tom Brown's Schooldays* was published in 1857, the year of Grace's first innings, and its author Thomas Hughes, muscular Christian and Christian socialist, made it the embodiment of fair play.

H. H. Almond, head of Loretto, was the one whose long reign inaugurated the open windows, cold showers and long runs which were, in part, the public school's contribution to the public health movement and what *Punch* mourned as 'England's perpetual bath-night'. Almond argued that games, rather than prohibitions, were the answer to the old obsession with hunting and shooting, and felt they taught self-reliance. It was in this vein that the notion of physical fitness overlapped with that other major Victorian concept—rampant individualism. This spread into the field of education and the professions.

'Rivalship and emulation render excellency' said Adam Smith, while, in a characteristic phrase, Jeremy Bentham said exams were a means of 'maximising aptitude'. James Booth, protagonist of examinations, claimed that examinations meant promotion 'by competition rather than conspiracy'. In 1859 Samuel Smiles published *Self-help*, his celebrated and hagiographical collection of engineering biographies.

In that same year Charles Darwin's *On the Origin of Species* was published, an endorsement, as far as many were concerned, of competitiveness and manliness. Herbert Spencer held that the healthy body must precede intellectual exercise. He coined the phrase 'survival of the fittest', a text for the competitive society. A healthy mind in a healthy body: Spencer preached the gospel of games, and society was keen to heed him. It was like a new religion. It was a mixture of non-conformist conscience, Christian muscularity, public health reform, self-reliance, business ethics and the new scientific beliefs. Cricket was the ideal expression. It was a clean-cut game which could promote fitness, honourable dealings and independence of spirit. Grace was often to be compared with the crusading knight, yet William Clarke—and Grace himself—were also exponents of Smilesian self-help. No wonder the public schools and universities took eagerly to cricket. In 1861, at Lord's, 700 carriages and ten times as many spectators rolled up for the first day of the Eton and Harrow fixture and several other schools—Repton, Uppingham, Cheltenham, Clifton among them—were running successful XIs.

At all levels, the cricketer was becoming regarded as the Christian at play, from a parish parson such as the Rev. John Dann, W.G.'s tutor, disporting himself on the village green, to C. T. Studd, of Cambridge University, Middlesex and England (five Tests in 1882), who, as a missionary twice-over, carried Christianity and cricket into the heart of China. Needless to say, the public schools and universities were staffed by and, in profusion, produced clergymen. These cricketing parsons fought degeneracy with the code of the playing field. Football, perhaps more so than cricket because of its simpler structure and equipment, was to be another saviour of the working classes. As in cricket, the move from a group activity to an inter-group competition led to a codification of the laws. The Football Association and the Salvation Army were both formed in 1863, and it was no coincidence, for both were concerned to save the poor through good works.

They were helped by the struggle to provide public playing areas. Social commentators such as R. A. Slaney had in the 1830s drawn attention to the loss of common land and its effect on health. In 1833 a Select Committee of the House of Commons on the deficiency of 'Public Walks and Places of Exercise' lamented that the growing towns offered no provision for 'the means of healthy exercise or cheerful amusement'. The twin thrust of expanding housing and agriculture robbed the lower classes of many of the traditional playgrounds, and the harassment of those trying to find a spot for games was yet another strain on the urban and, increasingly, the rural poor. The Health of Towns Commission, which reported in 1844, received evidence that the inhabitants of Basford (in that then bountiful county of cricketers, Nottinghamshire) had no land for play. This was, it claimed, 'a fruitful source of bickering and recrimination between the young men of the parish and the owners and occupiers of land, trespassers . . . for the purpose of cricket-playing and other games, being very common'.

But there had to be opportunity of time as well as of space. In the middle of the century the Short Time Central Committee coordinated the struggle to free workers to enjoy the new amenities. 'Parks are well', they argued, 'for those only who have time to perambulate them.' It was 'a mere burlesque upon philanthropy' to have parks with operatives working too long to benefit from them. Gradually, the Saturday half-day was introduced, and the Ten Hours Act was passed in 1847. By 1860, for instance, it was said that in the newly acquired Macclesfield park as many as forty cricket matches were played on a Saturday afternoon after the mills had closed.

Although young W.G. endured neither the rigours of the public school nor the arduous strain of the workshop, his formative years were spent in this new climate. Cricket spread on a nationwide basis on two levels. There was, so to speak, the topographical level with more and more clubs and more and more people playing the game at a higher and more consistent standard, and playing fixtures at greater distances. The South Wales club would play the Sussex Gentlemen at Brighton, or W.G. would, oddly, find himself travelling north to captain the Nottingham and Sheffield Colts. But, as important, there was what might be called the cultural, even the moral, level. There was the profound belief that, as moral succour for the workers or ethical practice for the upper and middle classes, cricket had this formidable recommendation that it was a virtuous game. It was W. G. Grace's good fortune, as its supreme proponent, to discover himself at the onset of his career just when cricket was becoming, geographically and socially, a major and abiding national interest.

# 3
# Grace as a Young Man and the Genesis of County Cricket (1866-73)

The Grace family was at this juncture faced with a predicament, but not one wholly displeasing to them. Their strapping son W.G. had, by his eighteenth summer, realised their fondest wishes and was, beyond all but the most pessimistic doubts, destined for greatness. The doubts were probably never more pessimistic than in the late winter of 1867 when he suffered a debilitating attack of scarlet fever. It was an age, of course, when scarlet fever, after cholera, typhoid and smallpox, was the most feared disease. For six weeks he was very ill, but rallied splendidly and what pneumonia appeared to have done for his batting four years before, scarlet fever now managed for his bowling. Although further reduced by the ill-luck of a sprained ankle and then a split finger, he took 131 wickets, and personally considered 1868 'his best bowling year'. He took eight for 25 for the Gentlemen versus the Players and six for 15 for England versus Middlesex; 39 of the wickets were first-class in 200 overs at an average of 7, and, although he did not score a century and had only five first-class innings, *Lillywhite's Almanac* felt able to describe him 'as a host in himself' and as 'a splendid fielder and thrower from leg'.

If W.G. wracked by misfortunes could so disport himself, what might he not achieve in full health? All believed that the phenomenon should be indulged and that W.G. should devote himself wholeheartedly to cricket—otherwise what point the colossal investment in time and energy? But Henry Grace Senior was just a typical country general practitioner of average income, with a couple of servants only and a sizeable family to raise. He could not afford to sustain his brilliant child over what was likely to be a long career. Moreover, he did not wish to leave his fourth son bereft of financial props should family fortunes falter or when he needed to earn a comfortable living as a domesticated person himself. The first three sons were well settled. Henry Junior was at Kingswood Hill, while Alfred, playing little cricket now but concentrating on his superb horsemanship, had qualified as a doctor in the early 1860s and had taken up his life-long attachment to the nearby Chipping Sodbury practice. In 1865 E. M. Grace obtained in turn his medical qualification—MRCS in England, and LRCP of Edinburgh. After a couple of years in Marshfield, a village east of Bristol, he moved to Thornfield. There he became Surgeon to the Workhouse, Parish Medical Officer and Public Vaccinator for forty years, and, in 1875, he was to become Coroner for East Gloucestershire: hence his later soubriquet of 'the Coroner' on the cricket field.

Until that point E. M. Grace had bid fair to be England's crack cricketer, a status dependent on such marathon achievements as the one in 1862, which he himself called 'the greatest of all my great performances', when he carried his bat for MCC against the Gentlemen of Kent, scoring 192, as a preface to taking all the Kentish wickets with his slow underhands. By now, however, his younger brother's shadow had begun to lengthen. The teenager's prowess and the distractions of a new medical practice were added to the probable flaw of his exciting but perverse unorthodoxy. The Rev. James Pycroft, that guarded critic of the period, warned that despite 'an energy and concentration of quickness and power which leaves nothing to be desired as regards a hitting game' Edward Miles Grace's 'facilities are apt to betray him'.

Fred Grace was now seventeen and beginning to show elegant promise. Like W.G., he had played against men at nine and had been infant prodigy enough to obtain thirteen wickets, but his teens had been less successful than the older brothers. He was seventeen before he made his first-class debut—for the North versus the South of the Thames in 1867—which he followed with his first game at Lord's for an England XI against the MCC. Here was another cricketing talent to be nurtured.

It is not clear how conscious the decision was, or whether, which is likely, it happened like so many domestic decisions, piecemeal, over the years, in sporadic reaction to changing conditions. But William Gilbert began his medical studies at the age of nineteen at the Bristol Medical School. He was, of course, a day student and the schedule was presumably a leisurely one, for it never inhibited him from pursuing a relentless round of cricket at all levels. There was talk of Caius College, Cambridge, while, at much the same time, Canon E. E. Carter, a cricket enthusiast from Yorkshire, so far put national honour before his shire's pride as to offer to arrange a place at Oxford for W.G. Henry Grace's insistence on his son following in the family profession and some anxiety about the funding of a university place were possibly matched by his doubts about Varsity cricket. It was dominated by the three cricketing schools, Eton, Harrow and Winchester, and until the 1860s, was happy-go-lucky and haphazard while most of the college cricket was jumbled together untidily on Cambridge's Parker's Piece or Oxford's Cowley Common. Henry Grace would not have been wrong in judging that his son's genius might more profitably be nursed at home.

W.G. probably accepted this with his usual good sense. None of his family were university men, so he had no immediate grounds for disgruntlement. Whether in the longer term this lack of university gilding, as well as the earlier absence of the public school imprimatur, rankled is less certain. In his later manhood both tokens were more highly prized, assuredly in a cricketing sense, and there were precious few of W.G.'s fellow amateurs who failed to boast a vintage school and university college besides their county in those illuminating brackets after their name.

Such times and occasions were, however, far off. Henry Grace faced the prospect of a lengthy war of attrition, its objective the capture of a medical qualification. Not instinctively sophisticated and quick-witted a scholar, his son was embarked on a slow voyage of study which was to last no less than twelve years until the safe harbour, an Edinburgh medical licentiate, was reached. Henry Grace had to ensure that both sporting enterprise and medical training could be economically underwritten, and it must have been hereabouts that a tacit decision was taken that W.G. would, without actually entering the professional ranks, accept whatever payments might reasonably be forthcoming from cricket. Victorian social barriers made hypocrisy difficult to dodge. It was difficult for a doctor's son to become a 'player' or, for that matter, live in the accustomed manner on the professional's meagre rewards. There was no way the family could sponsor W.G., let alone E.M. and G.F.

What W.G. did was, at least in England, to play as a first-class amateur and a second-class professional. He was soon to become the most popular attraction of the United South of England (later the United England) XI which Edgar Willsher, the controversial Kent

over-arm bowler, had formed in 1865. The halcyon days of exhibition
cricket were over, and the existence of seven 'circus' XIs had contributed to this decline by diluting public interest and private profits
alike. Chiefly because of Grace's frequent presence, the United
Southern England XI survived the longest, until 1882, but the late
1860s saw the end of Clarke's invention as an important force.

Grace played for payment under the strictest contractual terms, as
did other amateurs in the same straits, including his brothers. Indeed
Fred Grace was later to be omitted from a Gentlemen's XI on those
very grounds of having transgressed by being paid by the United
South. That W.G. was never threatened in this fashion is at once a
tribute to his enormous merit and a condemnation of the cant-ridden
standards of his peers. By the early 1870s, it was W.G. Grace who was
responsible for collecting the team and paying the players, while he
received a stated sum, match for match, legally observable and with a
penalty clause to cover his unavoidable absence. These were the times
when Grace's presence doubled the gate-money from sixpence to a
shilling, and Grace was as much the beneficiary as anyone. Given the
reduction in interest in these matches and the fact that no one could
match William Clarke's entrepreneurial astuteness, W.G. probably
rarely equalled 'old under-arm's' takings, but at an estimated £50
and more a game he would have, in terms of value, approached the
earnings per match of many a modern footballer.

With such humdrum matters reasonably well accommodated,
Grace proceeded to hurry through a number of seasons kaleidoscopi-
cally, his triumphs a seemingly endless burst of colour and vitality.
The beard was now growing towards its familiar bushiness and the
ample girth—he was 15 stones in his early twenties—had also
developed. It was a huge and distinctive presence, and, in the half-a-
dozen seasons remaining of his bachelordom and predating his first
and epic tour of Australia, his attainments surpassed the most inven-
tive flights of sporting fiction.

In retrospect, it does seem a packed and frantic time of cricketing
passion and exhilaration. Time has not lent much perspective to those
scenes. One knows that dreary winters intervened, with Grace
endeavouring to shut out the memories of cheering, sun-basked
crowds as he endeavoured to catch up with his medical studies. One
knows that there were the beagles to follow and the guns to shoot.
There was even a little rugby behind the Hen and Chickens public
house at Bedminster, but injury frightened him off, reminding him
sternly of his first duty, to remain hale and well for cricket.

Still the broken records and unprecedented statistics tumble over one another as one revisits those exciting seasons. One can do little more than catalogue the outstanding items, leaving in the miscellaneous columns performances which of themselves would have ensured another cricketer a revered place in the game's narrative.

In 1868, when just twenty, W. G. Grace played what he thereafter called 'my finest innings'. On a pitch playing—his own choice of adverb—'queerly' he battled against a dangerous Players' assault to score 134, all run, out of the Gentlemen's meagre 201 at Lord's. Only one other double-figure score was recorded in that innings. No one else topped 30 in the match on a wicket extremely perilous even by the Lord's yardstick and, with bowling figures of ten for 81, he won the game more or less single-handed. He followed this with the first twin centuries—130 and 102 not out for the South versus the North of the Thames at Canterbury—since William Lambert had managed a century in each innings at Lord's in 1817, and this was only the second time this had ever been achieved. He was mooted 'the best man in England' and it was about this time he was first referred to as 'the father of English cricket', with the malapropic addendum of 'and the brother of Dr E. M. Grace'.

The following year, when he celebrated his twenty-first birthday, that somewhat youthful 'father' astonished his disciples still further. He welcomed his majority with a series of nine centuries with the first, 177, against an Oxford University which dearly wished he had taken the Rev. Carter's advice. He scored 122 out of 169 (and took six for 52) for South against North, defiantly refusing to be budged by the likes of George Freeman and his insidious in-swingers or Tom Emmett and his testing speed. Then he raced to 180 for the Gentlemen of the South versus the Players of the South, his lion's share of a first-wicket partnership of 283, accumulated in not much over three hours.

In 1870 Grace remorselessly harried the Players again. His 215 at the Oval was the highest score in those matches and the first double-century. He also scored a century in the return game at Lord's and the Gentlemen delightedly extended their victorious reign. That double-century included, in those boundary-less days, an 8 and three 5s. But the nine centuries of 1870 were topped by the ten of 1871, the season Grace described years afterwards as 'my most successful year'.

It was a dreadful summer. The rain fell and, when it relented, chill breezes made the cricketers shiver. Grace was undaunted. An extraordinary factor in a game riddled with chance vulnerability was his assurance in making promises good. Twice in benefit matches, he was dismissed for nought in the first, only to make devastating amends in the second innings. After a duck—Shaw was the bowler—in H. H. Stephenson's benefit at the Oval, South against North, he struck a chanceless and gigantic 278. Bowled third ball by his old adversary, Shaw, in John Lillywhite's benefit match, Gentlemen against Players at Brighton, he corrected the balance with 217, his brother Fred and he racing to 240 in two and a half hours. On his first visit to Trent Bridge he chafed at his relative failure—79 out of Gloucester's 140. 'I will do it next innings', he announced and 116 out of 210 was the consequence, the first 'county' century on that famous ground. All in all, he totalled almost 6,000 runs in all games in 1871, while his first-class average, 78 from 2,739 runs, was twice as good as the trailing second in the table, the excellent Dick Daft on 39, an average which four years before would have been recorded as remarkable. It was the first occasion 2,000 first-class runs had been scored by anybody in one season.

By those standards 1872 was not quite so exciting. There were eight centuries and 4,500 runs and 170 for England against an extremely strong Notts and Yorks combine. Carrying cricket's banner to Glasgow with the USEE he hit a rollicking 114, striking the same 'sweet, unoffending lady' twice and landing one ball in a cab. Perhaps his most cherished achievement, however, was his characteristic response to Tom Emmett's gritty but untimely warning: 'Wait until we get him to Sheffield.' His 150 (all-run, with two 6s, a 5, eleven 4s and eighteen 3s) and fifteen for 79 was no bad haul for a first visit to Bramhall Lane. It was not the last time the Yorkshiremen were to suffer.

Taking stock of the years of W.G.'s first flush of maturity is a bewildering task. In the five seasons, 1868-72, he scored 21,628 runs in 388 innings at an average of 55. In one or two seasons he managed a hundred innings. In what were then regarded as first-class matches his average was just on 63—7,940 runs and 126 innings. Possibly those plain statistics tell the most lucid story. Cricket was suddenly a game in which larger numbers were bandied about. It was as if today the nation's premier football team started winning 9 or 10-nil every Saturday. And that is without brief mention of his dozens of enthusiastically taken wickets and his vim in the outfield. His venom with the bat sometimes makes one forget that he was the most feared amateur bowler of the day.

The plaudits came as thick and fast as the runs. *Lillywhite's*

*Cricketer's Companion*, the cricketer's bible of the time, agreed that he 'was generally admitted to be the most wonderful cricketer that ever held a bat'. *The Daily Telegraph* informed its readers that 'batting so triumphantly superior to all kinds of bowling brought against it has never been witnessed in our generation'. Some of the lovingly nursed folk-lore dates from that era. It was supposedly at Sheffield in 1872, apropos of W.G.'s 150, that the disconsolate Emmett said 'He dab 'em but seldom, and when he do dab 'em, he dabs 'em for four.' It was Tom Emmett who christened him, with primitively cryptic precision, a 'nonsuch', opining 'He should be made to play with a littler bat.' It was Alfred Shaw, whose honour it was to have so many Grace dismissals—twenty-one to his name—who, as Grace struck the 'sweet unoffending lady' and equally inoffensive cab while batting at Glasgow, answered a question about the master's gift. 'Well young gentleman, it's like this', he is reported to have, 'with a sailor-like hoist of his breeches and a grim smile', replied, 'I puts the ball where *I* pleases and Mr Grace puts it where *he* pleases.' *The Daily Telegraph* could not resist: of his 278 in Stephenson's benefit, it said 'Mr Gilbert Grace has outgraced himself.' Simply, this was the time when he was, just in his twenties, first given the unreserved title 'the Champion Cricketer', by *Lillywhite's Companion*.

These deeds were accomplished, it must be stressed, on dangerous pitches, sometimes without benefit of boundaries, against the then normally hurricane bowling, and, in less than first-class matches, frequently against fields as plentiful as twenty-two. The hazards of the fast bowler are not twentieth century in origin. It was only when Summers was tragically killed with that blow on the temple in 1870 that the heavy roller was introduced to help tame vicious wickets. George Freeman and Tom Emmett, doughty bowlers both, wondered at Grace's audacious power. 'It was a wonder', said the latter in later years, 'that the doctor was not either maimed or unnerved for the rest of his days or killed outright.' After a long innings against them, Grace's thigh was so pounded, that it resembled 'a mutton chop'.

He was not badly hurt because his clarity of eye and assurance of judgement matched his extraordinary strength and emotional poise. Beyond that, his unswerving courage equalled his formidable stamina. Day in, day out, with hours of batting, and an interwoven schedule of uncomfortable and tiring travel to boot, it is possibly the sheer physical fortitude and mental concentration which is most amazing. And for many years he retained an energetic interest in athletics. Many cricket clubs, like Bedminster or Oakfield, organised sports, while road races were very common. The Zoological Gardens, Clifton, was the chief arena for large-scale meetings in the west, and Grace and his relations entered for events in the annual Bristol, Clifton and West of England Athletic Festival. It was at the Berkeley Hunt point to point in 1867 that W.G. pulled off his celebrated law-and-order coup, when he hunted and harried a pickpocket across the fields and back into the arms of the local constabulary—a hue and cry which involved leaping 'a formidable looking iron gate' before the villain was recaptured by his—the local paper's phrase—'astonished custodian'.

One cloud marred his skies, however. Two days before Christmas, in 1871, his father died. He was sixty-three, and, to the last, he had kept up his interests in his patients and his cricketing brood alike. He had been a seriously religious man and a busy doctor, and he had, within his lights, proved to be a committed family man as well as a country sportsman of some merit. His death naturally saddened his family but it emphasised for his son how, with the family breadwinner departed, economic matters were (as perhaps H. M. Grace foresaw) more pressing. The following spring and summer witnessed W.G. playing much more frequently for the United South exhibition team.

Henry Grace survived long enough to be cheered by his son's unparalleled achievement, his last summer proving to be one of W.G.'s finest ever. He also left another legacy of substantial proportion in that he created the Gloucestershire County club.

The county pattern is so familiar that one tends to assume its longevity, but in historical terms, its complete predominance is little more than a century old. The relative novelty of fullscale county competition is all the more peculiar granted the claim for the first ever county match: Kent versus Surrey, 1709. Yet it took nigh on two hundred years to consolidate that early start. In the sporadic way of Georgian England thirteen counties fielded sides during the eighteenth century, but their geographical incidence is more interesting than their eventual quality, for only eight became first-class counties. What they illustrate is the south-eastern nature of the early game and its all but total dependence on London and London society.

During the reign of the entrepreneurial professionals, like Clarke and Wisden, county cricket merely limped along. The MCC played matches against the counties but this was perhaps because the MCC, frustrated by the public preoccupation with the touring teams, had not much alternative opposition. Still, it meant that county organisation, with the use of certain grounds and certain groups of professionals, was sustained, and there was a popular but arbitrary view of which was, each season, the most successful county. But this was no more than the kind of critical acclaim which suggested, say, that one rugby union club was superior to the others in the days before merit tables and cup competitions. As late as 1872 only twenty-five actual county matches were recorded for the season. But in the 1860s professional cricket was split. Rivalry between the circus sides was the undertow of much of this, with annoyance over the appointment of Surrey's Stephenson as the captain of the 1862 touring side to Australia an occasion for an overt quarrel. The rift was symbolised by a violent confrontation of the two leading groups from each camp, Nottinghamshire and Surrey, and the great North v South and All-England v United All-England fixtures, high points of any season, lapsed. Yorkshire, just beginning to demonstrate signs of its potential supremacy, was particularly to suffer from the schism.

The counties revived and began to fill the vacuum. In 1873 MCC flirted with a county knock-out cup. The year before the FA Challenge Cup had been first fought over, and, among much cross-matching of officers, it is worthy of recall that C. W. Alcock, first secretary of the FA and its cup's originator, was also secretary of Surrey. This notion was shelved because all matches were scheduled for Lord's and, after injuries in the Kent/Sussex tie, no one else would play and because it was feared gambling would be resumed. It was shelved for a conservative ninety years until, in 1963, the Gillette Cup was put up for competition, but MCC had had to consider the question of qualification. With players trudging up and down the country searching for the most profitable billet, there was a need, if competition was to have meaning, for some rules of eligibility.

Initially, it was determined that a player should play for but one county in any one season. For the first time—July 1873—there was some form of league under clearly defined rules of qualification and Gloucestershire shared the title with the Nottinghamshire of Dick Daft and Alfred Shaw.

Henry Grace was a pioneer to the point of zealotry of county cricket, and, as early as 1862, engineered a somewhat casual game between Gloucestershire and Devon. The West Gloucestershire club was, in the first place, a small-scale amalgamation and, more or less, the Bristol area representative team, but Henry was determined to take it further. His affection for county cricket was, naturally enough, sharpened by the fact that his talented sons had to travel at least as far as London to play in first-class matches. It was 1870 before W.G. played at home in a first-class match.

Before that, in June 1863, the Gentlemen of Gloucestershire visited Lord's, beating the MCC by 131 runs. This, however, was placed in harsh perspective the following month when twenty of Clifton including four Graces were mercilessly thrashed by the All-England XI, with Tarrant and Emmett sharing the forty victims, and W.G.'s 26 being the top score. The next year, the season when, at twenty-one, W.G. was granted membership of the MCC, a sure token of his accepted amateur status, there was more excitement at Clifton. There had just previously been a row on the field at the Oval involving Grace and the Lancashire bowler, Crossland, whose ill-repute ran both to body-line intimidations and throwing. His first delivery bounced straight at the local hero's head, and pandemonium ensued. W. G. Grace—no more than twenty-one, it should be stressed—threatened to clear the ground if the noise continued. The mob silenced, he proceeded to deal, as ever, with the enemy in the most productive manner, namely by hitting 112 solid runs.

Such ventures, however, were nothing without proper financial backing. Throughout 1869 and into the early months of 1870, the old doctor worked and worked, meeting the local gentry, arguing and debating with them on his single-minded objective, the establishment of a county club. At last, after years of disappointment at the impoverished attitude of Gloucestershire's leading sportsmen, a tiny list of three fixtures was arranged for the 1870 season.

On 2 June in that year Gloucestershire played its opening first-class match against Surrey on Durdham Down. The home county defeated its illustrious opponents by 51 runs, and, while managing only a couple of 20s with the bat, W.G. had a match analysis of nine for 96. As so often, his riposte to an apparent failure was as magnificent as his sense of occasion. The county played its other two games in London. In the return match at the Oval Surrey were destroyed in a couple of days by the long margin of an innings and 139 runs. W.G. scored 143 and took eight for 55. Then the MCC were summarily dispatched by an innings and 88 runs, with W.G. weighing in with 172 (out of 276) and seven for 65. Gloucestershire and its gifted proponent had arrived dramatically on the county scene.

H. M. Grace died, then, with his dual ambitions realised. In the next three seasons Gloucestershire consolidated that sturdy position. Surrey suffered again. In their second innings they were dismissed for 94, E. M. Grace six for 36, and his brother W.G. picking off the others, four for 17. To underpin the family contribution, Edward and Fred had six catches in that innings. In 1872 seven matches were played, with only one loss, and, with volcanic suddenness, here was Gloucestershire, the Johnny-come-lately, challenging the well-established leaders, like Yorkshire and Nottinghamshire. More formally, the first official documents of the club are dated 1873, and there are evident signs of institutionalised traits. The Duke of Beaufort, whose hounds the Graces had for many years followed, was the first president, and Lord FitzHarding was a vice-president. E. M. Grace began his long and diligent stint as secretary, and his brother Henry was a committee man. Needless to say, W.G. was skipper. Subscriptions for this new and exciting club were 10s annually, or £1 for the family; 5 guineas bought life-membership.

It must have seemed a cheap price to pay as, in that year, Gloucestershire were unbeaten and officially declared joint county champions. They won four and drew the other two of their half-a-dozen games. They beat Yorkshire twice, and Fred Grace, now regarded as England's second-best amateur and finest outfielder, scored 165 not out against them at Clifton. W. R. Gilbert, a cousin of the Graces, made some runs, and there was the adventurous Frank Townsend, J. A. Bush, the most competent amateur wicket-keeper of the period, and the talented off-spinner, R. F. Miles, to keep the Graces handsome and entirely amateur company. How pleased the old doctor would have been to have watched over his sons organising and leading England's now premier county, only three years since that opening game against Surrey.

Gloucestershire's rise was remarkably similar in character to several of its fellow counties, for one of the truisms of cricket history is that county unification is frequently club expansion. Surrey, for example, is the child of the Montpelier CC, for no sooner had the club moved to Kennington in 1845 than a general meeting of Surrey cricketers was called to establish a county presence. A few years earlier Sussex had coordinated the county effort around its traditional focus of Brighton. Middlesex was as late as 1877 before it commenced its famous acquaintance with Lord's, having had previous homes in Islington and Southgate.

Earlier, Kentish cricket had based itself on Canterbury and Maidstone, both close to seats of its patron, Sir Horatio Mann. Yorkshire was the creation of Sheffield cricket, as Lancashire was of Manchester's. In 1857, at a cost of £1,000, the Manchester club moved to the present Old Trafford site and in January 1864 convened a meeting to decide how best to form a county club.

The formation of the first-class counties is also marked by the intervention in each case of one or more energetic and influential mentors in direct line of descent from the old-time patrons of whom H. M. Grace is a fine example. Others included the Rev. G. L. Langdon for Sussex; William Ward and the Hon. Fred Ponsonby for Surrey; Ponsonby's friend, Bob Grimston and I. D. Walter for Middlesex; 'Monkey' Hornby for Lancashire; and, most famously, Lord Hawke for Yorkshire and Lord Harris for Kent—these, and others, were the men who paternalistically guided their counties into the top rank.

Only Gloucestershire could, however, boast a W. G. Grace to command them and 1873 proved to be another spectacularly successful year for him. Returning from a brief tour of Canada in the winter of 1872, he proceeded to score six centuries and total 2,139 runs in first-class cricket, the second time he had reached that second thousand. He went a stage beyond that. He took 100 wickets for the first time (106, to be exact) and, in so doing, became the first cricketer ever to achieve the 'double'—a thousand runs and a hundred wickets. His average was 71, and he scored another 2,431 in second-class matches. His leading performances were 192, undefeated, for South versus North, and 163, including a 7, against the long-suffering Players, and, further testimony to his monopoly of an innings, 145 out of 237 against the Players of the North.

In 1872 W. G. Grace had met and paid court to the daughter of a first cousin, William Day of Colehan Road, South West London. The courtship had proceeded in that elaborate and ritualistic manner beloved of the Victorian gentry and their wives, and no doubt the families played a part. The Graces and their offshoots by affinity or marriage, like the Pococks, Gilberts and Days, were a close-knit and clannish lot, much given to largish domestic gatherings. They all met frequently and socially, and the friendship between Agnes Nicholls Day and W. G. Grace evidently deepened into an affection welcome on all sides. On 9 October 1873, they were married at St Matthias Church, West Brompton. The Rev. John Dann, W.G.'s tutor and brother-in-law, officiated, with two other vicars in support, while J. A. Bush, the Gloucestershire wicket-keeper, was best man.

There is little to suggest that W. G. Grace, despite his keenness for dancing, was much of a ladies' man. No scandalous titbits of gossip have survived about a man who after all, travelled widely and was as widely fêted wherever he travelled. There seem to have been no major romances in early manhood, nor yet any passionate affairs in later life. The rightness of the marriage has about it an almost artificial Victorian punctiliousness. Agnes and Gilbert were of the same generation, family and social class. She was of pleasing and placid disposition, with a temperament equable enough to tolerate and complement the sometimes overspirited outbursts and the hyperactive doings of her spouse. A dark, buxom girl of prepossessing looks and habits, she has been described as 'highly competent'. Certainly she was a well-organised housewife and mother, but little of passion and sensuality leaps over the years to excite one's emotional instincts. It was, on both sides, a marriage dutifully observed according to the mores of the age, with W.G. in pursuit of sporting glory and allied pleasures, and Agnes content to superintend a never ostentatious home. However, it was not an unfeeling or a cheerless marriage but an amiable and highly workable alliance at a time when marriages were often cruel and crampingly restrictive. Yet it is difficult to avoid the impression that it happened inexorably as part of some ordained, bourgeois plan, the two coming together to fulfil their expectations, and that of their families, of how their social destiny should be played out. A further feature is the question of income. It was nearly two years since Henry Grace's death, and W.G. was not much advanced with his medical studies and assuredly had no employment other than as a paid cricketer. One possibility is that William Day, a man of well-to-do, but not extravagant, means, saw his way to providing something of a dowry or even a marriage settlement, and it is thought W.G. inherited a small legacy from his father. Certainly W.G. and Agnes enjoyed their six initial years of marital stability, until he qualified as a doctor, without any apparent financial problems.

It is clear enough that, somehow, their families and cricket between them sponsored the young giant's onward march; and a fortnight after these nuptials had been celebrated, the newly wed champion left with his bride for the famous honeymoon tour of Australia.

# 4
# Grace in Australia: The Colonisation of Cricket (1873/4)

The distance between England and Australia could scarcely have been longer, or the variation in climate and conditions more marked. Here was a land, huge, arid and inhospitable, and some two or three months voyage distant from England. Yet it was to be the second great fount of modern cricket. Whereas English cricket can, if a trifle romantically, be traced back to medieval times and earlier, Australia and Australian cricket was immediate and sudden in its arrival on the historical scene. In 1787 the MCC was formed. In the same year eleven ships sailed under the command of Captain Arthur Philip for Australia. They arrived in the January of 1788, and white Australia dates from that time. Chiefly under the pressure of providing accommodation for convicts, the colony expanded swiftly. The recent loss of the American colonies in 1783 was a spur, for, convicts apart, there was a need to look for new trading posts and potential spots for settlement.

About fifty years later Charles Darwin visited Australia and glowingly admired its 'converting vagabonds, most useless in one hemisphere, to active citizens of another'. This was fairer comment than those who saw Australia as no more than a penal sink, but the fittest who survived there did so in conditions of some difficulty. Even so the natural instinct of the émigré seems to be to preserve the values of home. A constant theme throughout colonialism is this tendency, in a purportedly new life, to ensure that nothing of the old is lost. Certainly the Australians commenced to out-Herod Herod. Throughout the nineteenth century and into the twentieth, many of them conserved and sustained a bizarre Englishness. Almost immediately as well as musical evenings, balls and horse-riding, there was cricket.

In the first sixty years of the Australian story, everything seemed to conspire to make a niche for cricket. English cricket, in its early modern form, was chiefly an urban, indeed, in first-class terms, a chiefly London game. Australia's two great new cities, like London, quickly became cricketing centres of unquestionable import. All in all, cricket survived its transplantation to Australia with impressive ease, because, by accident and by design, Australia was initially a little England. But there was, as yet, no sense of cricket identity between the two countries, no exchange of cricketers or cricket matches between the two, not least because Australia was, to English eyes, in no way a country. That development, which was to carry cricket into its oceanic and international stage, was to follow hard on the events which transformed Australian life in mid-century.

Early in 1851, a small strike in New South Wales led to the Australian gold rush. By December of that year, there were 20,000 'diggers' on site. In 1852, 300 ships sailed for Australia, and in 1853 nigh on a thousand boats made the journey, some of them now sailing from Germany, the United States and China. In a couple of years Victoria's population sprang from 77,000 to 170,000 and was already marginally bigger than New South Wales.

Among the thousands who, messing in tens or dozens in the squalid confines of the battered emigrant ships, were thus tempted was a Gloucestershire man called William John Midwinter. He was from Chedworth, near Cirencester, and his wife Rebecca Evans was a farmer's daughter from St Briavels. It was in that same village in the Forest of Dean that their son William was born on 19 June 1851. It was just three years after the birth of W. G. Grace and the very year that the gold craze shook Australia. Ten years later John Midwinter, a restless and itinerant cove, with but some mining experience in the Forest of Dean to support him, embarked from Liverpool on the *Red Jacket* in February 1861. It was 24 April, a matter of twelve weeks, before Melbourne was reached by John and his wife, William and his brother John and sister Jean. It was the first of many such journeys that William Midwinter was to make.

During the 1850s its population more than doubled from less than half a million to over a million. Victoria, where the gold rush was located, alone had more than half-a-million inhabitants. At its centre was Melbourne, a typical immigrant city, heaving and crawling with humanity, vital and colourful yet full of hazards and pitfalls. No less than a third of its population lived in tents and clumsy huts. It was called 'the phenomenal city'; it had the authentic ring of Victorianism:

opulent riches and prestige buildings alongside abject impoverishment and floating sewage; a careful parade of Christian commitment
alongside brothels open twenty-four hours a day. In a decade, the gold
rush helped increase the tempo of demographic and urban extension.
And it was the concentration of larger populations in urban confines
which created modern spectator sports.

William Midwinter was brought up among the wildness and adventure of the Bendigo gold-field, and the family settled at California
Gully near Sandhurst (now known as Eaglehawk). Like so many tyro
goldminers, the father turned to a service trade. Drawing no doubt on
his sheep-farming background, he took up butchery, and helped equip
the prospectors with the mutton which, in a country which had 16
million sheep, was naturally their staple diet. William had some
schooling and assisted his father as a butcher's boy. In between times
he played cricket, and there was a canine fielder as in the young
Grace's Downend practices. There the domestic comparison ended.
Whereas the Graces lived in comfort and daily batted and bowled in
their orchard, the Midwinters, like hundreds of their neighbours in
the gold-fields, dwelt in a stone-floored, wooden shack, nearby which
they played what cricket they could. It was William's good fortune to
strike up a childhood friendship with Harry Boyle, some years his
senior, a man destined to be rated not only a sound player but a competent official in Australian cricket circles. Boyle played for Sandhurst
and William for California Gully School, but Harry Boyle organised—
and he was still in his teens—the Sydney Flat CC. This was a couple of
miles from Sandhurst, but he and a dozen or so other youngsters,
including 'Mid', grafted away to construct a pitch among the mine
workings. So successful were they that eight of them next played for the
district team, Bendigo United, with William, at thirteen, showing his
prowess at almost as youthful an age as the Champion. Imagine the
enthusiasm all this entailed. For eleven-year-old William, it was normally a round journey on foot of ten miles, not just to play, but to help in
levelling and clearing. Playing for Bendigo meant even more travelling, and much of it was straightforward hiking. William Midwinter
was typical of the emigrant stock which, particularly in Australia, was
determined to transfer the English traditions and was prepared to
match that determination with dynamic energy. The *Melbourne
Standard* praised his devotion. Having been employed by his butcher
parent 'occasionally with the basket', he toiled with his mates, by
moonlight, for weeks to tear a pitch from the bush land. Along with
the ten-mile tramp, it constituted 'proof of his early ardour'.

In the season 1869/70 (before his nineteenth birthday) 'Mid' became the first person to score a double century in Australian cricket, 256 for Bendigo versus his home-town club, Sandhurst. The Carlton Cricket Club, the premier Melbourne Club, were impressed by both Boyle and his younger friend. In 1872 they were two of the Bendigo VI which beat Charles Bannerman's New South Wales IV in a single-wicket contest. Much money was probably lost on this match, for the Bannerman quartet were obviously hot favourites. Soon both Boyle and Midwinter became prominent members of the Melbourne club side.

By this time the changes wrought by the gold rush had forged cricketing links between the old country and the new. The first overseas tour from England had been to North America, when, in 1859, a twelve-strong professional squad had endured appalling Atlantic crossings and almost as dreadful playing conditions (they fielded in great-coats at Hamilton in several inches of snow) to thrash five teams overwhelmingly. But it was the more 'English' and less cosmopolitan Australia, which was to dominate the overseas cricket scene. The Melbourne Cricket Club was formed in 1838 and the first inter-colonial match, resulting in a narrow defeat for Victoria at the hands of New South Wales, took place at the height of the gold rush in 1856.

Grace's first tour of 1873 had been preceded by two other trips. Two caterers, Felix Spiers and Christopher Ponds, who were busily making fortunes providing refreshments for the gold-miners, were responsible for the first. On Christmas Eve 1861, H. H. Stephenson and eleven fellow-professionals, mainly from Surrey, disembarked at Melbourne. Ten thousand Australians greeted them, and fifteen thousand watched their opening fixture on Melbourne's spacious ground with its magnificent pavilion and impressive grandstands, the first major cricket ground of the modern era. Each player wore a sash and a ribbon on his featherweight sun helmet, the colour corresponding to the key on the programme for ease of identification. The professionals earned £150 plus expenses, and Pond and Spiers made over £11,000 profit from the twelve-match tour.

Two years later, in 1863, George Parr (who, like one or two other northern 'pros', had jibbed at the 1861 voyage after the horrors of the American crossing) was persuaded, by Stephenson's triumph, by a first-class passage and a guarantee of £250, to lead a formidable combination to Australia. This was the tour E. M. Grace had joined and about which he wrote at the time in great detail and with an acute eye for Australia's 'bounceable' character. He spoke of the unique openings for venturesome enterprise, and also of how 'cricket reigned supreme' because 'everything which keeps them united to Britain and to Britain's green and to Britain's people, everything which binds them in any way close to those they left behind, is regarded with feelings of no ordinary pleasure'. Although XXII of New South Wales ran them extremely close, Parr's side survived the tour unbeaten. Charles Lawrence had, after the 1861/2 trip, remained behind as a coach, and, at the end of the 1863/4 tour, William Caffyn, who had been a stalwart on all three overseas programmes, began seven years sterling work as a coach, mainly with the Melbourne Club. Some commentators claim that his influence more than anyone's was responsible for the rapid improvement in Australian cricket. An unaccountable time passed. Charles Lawrence brought over to England his aboriginal cricketers who doubled as boomerang-throwers, in 1868, to the confusion of some Englishmen, who formed very strange views of Australian life and cricket. But it was not until the winter of 1873 that another English party set forth to Australia.

W. G. Grace had visited Canada and the USA the year before for a relaxing tour, despite suffering the foulest of seasickness aboard the SS *Sarmatian* on the outward and the SS *Prussian* on the inward journey. The games were easy, and W.G. contributed 540 of the 1,666 runs scored by the Englishmen. They had been invited by a Toronto businessman, Mr Pottieson, and the trip was organised by Fitzgerald, the secretary of MCC. This was the tour when W.G. invented the standing joke of his cryptic after-dinner speech. It ran 'I beg to thank you for the honour you have done me. I never saw better bowling than I have seen today, and I hope to see as good wherever I go.' By substituting 'better ground', 'prettier ladies', 'good fellows' and so on, he was able to exist as an orator on one all-embracing sentence. Hailed everywhere he went as, 'the Champion Batsman of Cricketdom and a monarch in his might', Grace was fêted and showered with gifts.

In Australia the standard of play and the tenacity of the players was much higher, however, than in the US and Canada. It was Melbourne Cricket Club which had, in the spring of 1873, issued the invitation, and it was W. G. Grace who organised the response. He groaned that he was 'heartweary' at his efforts to raise a side, but his niggardly terms—second-class passage and a miserly £170 fee—scarcely helped. Some professionals were offended and refused, leaving the party weakened by the absence of Emmett and Shaw among several others. However, James Lillywhite and Southerton (who was to take no less than 320 wickets) joined with the Gloucester amateurs, Fred

Grace, Bush and W. R. Gilbert in a mainly south of England group, and off they sailed in October.

The success of the tour was heavily dependent on W.G. To say the least, he was allowed very generous expenses, and a prolonged gratis honeymoon, courtesy of the Melbourne Cricket Club, was an extra- ordinary perquisite. But he had to play in every match, and, if a match finished early, he had to provide exhibition cricket. Maybe the inter- lock of Grace the drawcard and Grace the wage-earner fed the rumour that he had backed himself not to be bowled out on Australian soil. When in the opening match against Victoria, Harry Boyle clean bowled him, there was wild excitement. (F. R. Spofforth, incidentally, first came into prominence during this tour, when he bowled W.G. in the nets.) Assuredly there was betting involved in the cricket, all of which stimulated further interest, as it had done in earlier times in England and the telegraph was used to transmit scores for the very first time.

It is as well to stress the commercial character of these tours. This is not done cynically: as far as one can judge (and in spite of the fudging of the professional-amateur boundary) the enterprises were honestly, even courageously organised. There was probably some thought of spreading the gospel and bringing the faith to the primitives, but this was a secondary consideration. What it was not was international cricket. The English sides were not recognised as representative of the nation, and Australia was not yet regarded as a nation. The rivalry was there; it was personal and it was, increasingly, Englishman versus Australian. But it was not England versus Australia.

No one would deny that this was a most arduous venture. W. G. Grace, in rotund Victorian phrases, described some of the rigours in his memoirs. To begin with, the sea journey in 1873 took over seven weeks, on the *Mirzapare* to Ceylon and thence by the *Nabia*. Including the return journey, this meant fifteen weeks—nearly a third of the year—at sea, plenty of time for W.G. to indulge his devotion to whist. Then consider the following: the tourists had to travel from Ballarat to Stowell, a distance of seventy-four miles, over rough bush track. They travelled in a Cobb's coach, little more than an open cart, in pitiless heat through thick dust. Within minutes, they were 'up to the hocks' in choking white dust. The journey began at 8.30 am and it was 8.30 in the evening before Stowell was reached. The game began the following day on a field ploughed only three months earlier and upon which grass seed had been sown in honour of the English cricketers' visit. The match completed, despite a plague of flies, the tourists rose the following morning at 4.30 am and set off for Warrnambool. The first leg of this jaunt took them to Ararat, a journey of ninety-one miles. They may have conjectured wryly about Noah's connections with the original Ararat, for this trip was negotiated through torrential rain, with the sportsmen soaked utterly to the skin. The Cobb's coach found the mud of the Ararat track as impenetrable as the dust of the Stowell road, and it took twelve hours—not much more than seven miles an hour—to reach Ararat. After the briefest of respites, the remainder of the journey to Warrnambool was undertaken. This was thirty miles, again in atrociously muddy conditions, and over five hours elapsed before their destination was sighted, an average rate of six miles an hour. It was well-nigh midnight when the exhausted and half-drowned party arrived in Warrnambool, having spent nineteen hours on the road. Next day they had to be ready for cricket.

That was a difficult but not wholly unrepresentative week for W.G. and his compatriots. It must have been a test of the strongest of constitutions and it reads not unlike the narrative of some epic military exercise in one or other of Britain's African colonies. Opponents in such places as Stowell and Warrnambool were by no means top class and the Englishmen were constantly frustrated by bad pitches. According to Grace, a bushel of pebbles had to be collected from a wicket in Tasmania before play commenced.

Grace's party overcame these handicaps royally. They won twelve of the fifteen matches—all against odds—losing three, and W.G. had a batting average of 39 (758 runs) and took 65 wickets (average 7·4); his brother Fred was second in both bowling and batting. Perhaps the proudest performance was the defeat of a strong joint Victoria/New South Wales XV by 218 runs, while the Champion's own best feat was 126 against XVIII of Victoria. The crowds were phenomenal: 15,000 had turned up for the Victoria match, and 20,000 watched the English play the Ballarat XXII. The enthusiasm of the welcome was equally magnificent. Torchlight processions, troupes of dashing horsemen, mayoral receptions and stirring military bands were deployed to enliven their welcome, while the private hospitality was no less opulent. Grace recorded that he hunted rabbits, pigeons, kangaroo, quail, plover and goldfish, the last of which he ate and found 'very good, too'. The young Mrs Grace stayed with friends in the large cities while her untiring spouse stopped cricket only to start shooting, driving on bush tracks and tossing on coastal steamers in a ceaseless cycle of frenetic activity. It is typical of Grace—perhaps of the Victorian bourgeois male—that his honeymoon did not encapsu-late that brief phase of private passion and constant attention of the romantic definition.

The Australians were unstinting in their praise for W.G.—'a freak of nature, a cricket phenomenon' said the Melbourne press. Nonethe-less, there was considerable irritation and argument, and, indeed, that strange compound of affection and abrasiveness which has long characterised England/Australia cricket began at this juncture. Grace was not blameless. He was loud and contemptuous in his criticisms of pitches, although his brother Edward must have forewarned him. More justifiably, he took grave exception to the Australian practice of moving from a rough to a smooth pitch for the home team's innings. He was equally severe on umpires, growing all but choleric at those officiating when XXII of Castlemaine were the opposition. There was much talk of Australians failing to abide by umpiring decisions, and much of the antagonism was apparently personalised between Grace and the Australian cricketer and administrator, John Conway.

The Australians were much less genial than in the 1860s, improved standards and heightened aspirations having sharpened their game. They found Grace overbearing and petty, and they evid-ently judged him an ingrate apropos the hospitality urged upon him and the money that he was coining. One Australian newspaper summed it up at the end of the tour: 'Now it must be confessed, if only in a shamefaced fashion, that in Australia we did not take too kindly to W.G. For so big a man he is surprisingly tenacious on very small points. We duly admired him at the wicket, but thought him too apt to wrangle in the spirit of a duo-decimo attorney over small points of the game.' Fred Grace, the gentlest of the brothers but as fiercely loyal to the family name as any of them, was perhaps more sensitive to the atmosphere: 'We were met', he said dolefully in *Lillywhite's* the following year, 'in bad spirit, as if cricketers were enemies.' Perhaps another Australian report came closest to a summary text of this adventure. Of the game at Ballarat it briefly reported: 'The wicket played beautifully, the sun shone hotly; the XI scored tremendously; we fielded abominably; and all drank excessively.' Apart from the opening clause, it was a fair summation.

This was the time when Grace and Billy Midwinter crossed paths. Midwinter played twice for Victoria teams against Grace's team. In December 1873 he managed only 7, with Grace capturing his wicket. This was a three-day game watched by no less than 40,000 people. But some weeks later, in March 1874, he took 3 for 29, playing for a

Victoria XVIII. 'Amidst the greatest enthusiasm' (the *Melbourne Standard*'s phrase) he clean-bowled both W.G. and his brother G.F.

Did W. G. Grace make a 'pact', as Benny Green called it (in an article in *The Observer*, 'Not Quite Cricket'), with W. E. Midwinter, so that, were he to come back to England, he would play for Gloucester? Certainly Benny Green believes that he did, and W.G. would have realised that Midwinter was Gloucester-born. There was some confusion about this, for there were claims that he was a true-born Aussie. H. S. Altham, usually the model of precision, labels him a Canadian, just to add to the mystery. Possibly Midwinter was later content to appear under one label or the other as it suited his purpose. Of course, in the previous summer season, the MCC had tightened up its birth-qualification rules, and it may have occurred to Grace to put in a word to the wise. On the other hand, these were Gloucestershire's finest seasons: they were, defiantly, an all-amateur, all-conquering combine. And, had W.G. fancied Midwinter's assistance, there is no reason why he should not have found the emigrant all-rounder willing to return then rather than in 1877.

As it was, Agnes and W. G. Grace retraced their seaward steps without him, fifty days of intermittent *mal der mer* and hands of whist stretching from Adelaide until, on 18 May, Southampton was reached. It was an unhappy sort of trip for a honeymoon; there was, among the feasting and jollification, a little too much rancour. There had even been suggestions that Grace cheated in regard of his fees, and it was a full twenty seasons before he returned to Australia. The English were, in part, unpopular, just as the Australians were, in part, despised. At the same time, there was genuine admiration and friendliness on both sides. It was the start of a long and traditional rivalry, and W. G. Grace was, for good and ill, its chief progenitor. He was but a twenty-five-year-old medical student, but he bestrode the cricketing globe like a colossus.

# 5
# W. G. Grace and the County Championship (1874-6)

Grace returned to England an international as well as a national star. His hugely commanding physical presence, heightened by the fierceness of the thick, black beard, was now matched by a social maturity which was not wholly attractive. A gross and overwhelming confidence was perhaps the natural outcome of success, but there was a keenness just too finely honed and an outspokenness barely too short of rudeness for those of gentle manner. It was the Australian press, where 'the cry of sorrow is freely uttered' as E. M. Grace had put it, which was first and foremost in criticism of that brand, and the anecdotes of W.G.'s egocentric stubbornness and argumentativeness begin about this date and grow.

It was in the summer of 1874 that antagonisms flared in the Gentlemen and Players match. This concerned appeals by James Lillywhite for—those most divisive of umpiring decisions—obstruction and leg before wicket while Grace was batting, with Grace, as almost ever, overwhelmingly having his way. W.G. described the incident as 'one of the remarkably few instances of a difference of opinion between my opponents and myself', an interpretation Bernard Darwin suggested showed 'some economy of historical accuracy'. And in that way he had of adding injury to insult, the Gentlemen won and the two younger Grace brothers took all the wickets.

He was home, as man and as cricketer, with a vengeance. A winter had passed with precious little by way of medical studies and W.G. had to try and make amends over the next nine months. His attachment to the Bristol Medical School and Royal Infirmary remained, and, with increasing perseverance as autumn and winter circled yet again and another cricket season dwindled, he continued his studentship until the February of 1875, when, having finished his junior studies, he transferred to St Bartholemew's Hospital in London.

For those first few months of their married life, then, the young Graces joined the family homestead. They lived at the 'Chestnuts' with Mrs Grace, now in her sixty-first year. Luckily, Agnes Grace was an eager cricket fan, ever ready to watch her husband play or acquiesce in his constant absences on cricketing jaunts. It was as well, for Martha Grace's interest was unabated, and, until her death, she maintained logs and scrapbooks of all her sons' doings. It must have not been too comfortable sharing a house with the widow who doubled as her husband's mother and coach, and with one's husband devoted to the widow on both counts. 'Willie, Willie', she had been wont to chide him after a dismissal, 'haven't I told you over and over again how to play that ball.' Her sons took to telegraphing their scores to her from away games. One such wire read: 'From W. G. Grace, Huddersfield, to Mrs Grace, Downend. North 187, South, 2nd innings, 57, Self not out 35. Many Happy Returns of the Day.'

Fred Grace, for whom a medical career was also planned, was still at home, and the other brothers were exceedingly close by. Following Blanche, two more sisters had married, both, after that same social fashion of the age, doctors. After Alice had married Dr Bernard, Annie, even more typically, had become the wife of Dr Skelton, her father's assistant. This left Fanny, who remained a spinster, in the family nest to share the female duties with the young Mrs Grace. It must have been a trying induction for Agnes.

W.G. had by now abandoned his athletic career. It had been successful, although at sixteen he had managed, it was said, 'as poor a show as the mind of man can conceive'. As with cricket 'dogged perseverance' was the key, and for some years he was a thorough and competitive all-rounder, picking up a collection of first prizes, medallions and other trophies. As well as the quarter mile—his best event—he tried the hundred yards sprint, the two hundred yards hurdles, the long jump and the hop, skip and jump, and he threw the cricket ball 117 yards. By the time of his marriage, however, his gargantuan bulk had told. He was even too heavy to ride the one horse the household boasted but, typically, he followed the hounds on foot at a belligerent trot. His delight in the slaughter of the woodland population never lessened. He continued his interest in the Clifton and later the Worcester Park beagles and discovered a new interest in coursing. He treated partridge and woodcock with the same violence he meted out to bowlers. More sedately, he enjoyed like many another Victorian gentleman some billiards and later he found in the bicycle a sturdy substitute for the quadruped.

Grace's last summer in the maternal household was a satisfactory one. Early on he hit a massive 259 in a club game for Thornbury against Alveston. There were ten 6s and twenty-eight 4s. In all matches he scored over 5,000 runs, and, when he sailed over with the United South and scored 153 against XXII of Leinster, he had assembled the weird record of a century in England, Scotland, Australia, Canada and Ireland. He reached the hundred mark no less than a dozen times, including 179 against Sussex and—his usual trouncing of Yorkshire—167 at Sheffield, where he also finished with a match analysis of twelve for 104  Playing for MCC against Kent (with twelve men) he became the first cricketer to score a century (123) and perform the hat-trick (six for 47, following five for 82 in the first innings) in the same match. His best bowling in the county championship was fourteen for 66 against Surrey at Cheltenham.

The Gloucestershire county committee, was, as committees often are, heir to managerial tensions, many involving W.G. and his bellicose brother Edward. The elder brother, secretary of the club until 1909, was an autocratic administrator, but there were others ready to join battle with him. There was a squabble with Nottinghamshire over a fixture date, a row which involved W. G. Grace, and led to a couple of fractious meetings. 'After much conversation of not too polite a nature, as the Reverend J. Greene disputed the correctness of the notes taken by the secretary... saying that his memory was superior to the black and white testimony of the secretary', ran the relevant minute, while, at the next meeting, E.M. laconically recorded: 'Present: E M Grace, and that's all.' Apparently the Rev. J. Greene and his allies deliberately stayed away.

Such disharmonies were constantly to mar the smooth running of the county committee. Some time later, in a dispute over whether E. M. Grace might, as secretary, vote at committee meetings, the Rev. J. Greene, who chaired the proceedings, led a ten-man resignation. They were reinstated at the next meeting when, grudgingly, E.M. agreed not to vote, but four members of the eleven, Fenton Miles, Bush, who had been W.G.'s best man, F. Townsend and T. G. Matthews, were among them. One cannot doubt that the Graces' heavy-handedness in the organisation of the club was at least partially to blame for such dislocations. When, much, much later, the rupture between W.G. and the county occurred, it was the last straw rather than the first shell.

At this point, of course, the Graces were indispensable to Gloucestershire cricket, and the county won the title outright in 1874. After an opening defeat at Surrey's hands, albeit with the team much weakened, everything went well, and they triumphed readily in their home matches in high summer at Clifton College and Cheltenham. An innings victory over Surrey spelt out a special vengeance, the Londoners managing only 27 in their first innings at Cheltenham, and the Graces having more or less a hand in all the wickets. In five seasons of county cricket, Gloucestershire had shared the title once and won it outright once, and, in those five seasons, W.G. had scored over 2,000 runs for an average of 66 in some thirty innings.

Little wonder Gloucester paid him expenses. In the county committee minutes of 22 October 1874, a reimbursement of £45 to W.G. and £35 to G. F. Grace is recorded. It was not a fortune, although it was what the average bricklayer would then have earned in a year. It should also be recalled that no more than half-a-dozen or so matches were involved, and, despite their both living in the same place and presumably incurring similar expenses, the Grace brothers' expenses were rather different. E. M. Grace also took £60 each year for his secretarial expenses, although truth to tell, that was probably hard-earned. Gloucestershire was not, in spite of its immediate success, a well-supported county. In the following year, 1875, there were only seven people at the annual general meeting, proof, according to E. M. Grace, of 'how little interest subscribers take in county cricket'. It was an impoverished club, and the £140 paid out to the Grace brothers was, in relative terms, quite a hefty item. W. G. Grace was, however, a national figure, already displacing politicians of the day from the leader columns of the fashionable press. One spoke of 'grave propositions having been made in the higher councils of the craft—entreating that he will consent to play for the future either blindfolded or with his right arm tied behind his back'. *Punch* found in his familiar figure and colossal reputation endless sources for cartoon, versification and ponderously comic prose. In 1873, *Fun*, a contemporary of *Punch*, founded a mythical society 'for the Improvement of Things in General and the Diffusion of Perfect Equality'. Its agenda included such inhibiting propositions as 'that his shoe spikes shall be turned inward' or 'that he shall be declared out whenever the umpire likes', and, ultimately, 'that he shall not be allowed to play at all'.

Those who had scoffed at or feared for the late Henry Grace's presumption at forming a regular county side worthy of the illustrious might of Surrey or Nottinghamshire were silenced. Other critics were on safer ground when they pointed to the western county's over-reliance on the Grace trio. In the very August when Gloucestershire won its first championship, an anonymous letter, published locally, took up these particular cudgels. 'Why have we no professional players, with a reserve army of professional colts?' was the question. The writer was charmed by cricket's 'softening influence' and of the humour, for example, in watching 'a stout gentleman like Mr Bush slip, and, rolling over on his back, display his heels high in the air'. Here was fit commons for the workers. 'There are, I fancy, some Gloucestershire men who would be none the worse off if we could remove them from the tap-room into the more bracing atmosphere of Durdham Down.' This was a portentous warning only partially heeded, for, as the unknown commentator prophetically concluded, 'We depend, for the present, upon the Grace family; and, for the future, upon whatever the Colleges of Cheltenham and Clifton may chance to provide for us.'

But as of then the scene was a sunny one, and such pessimism seemed cantankerous and misplaced. Nor was all the rejoicing for sporting reasons. Agnes Grace was six months pregnant when she returned from Australia, and her sojourn at the 'Chestnuts' was broken by the birth of her eldest son. He took his father's Christian names exactly, and the new William Gilbert was born on 6 July 1874. Agnes's father was a lithographer who lived in the Clapham Common area, and his daughter returned home for her first lying-in—away, it might be noticed, from the several hearty country doctors who were her brothers-in-law. In February the Graces and their seven-month-old heir moved to London and took apartments in the Earls Court district, four or five miles from St Bartholomew's Hospital. At Bart's W.G. walked the wards under the supervision of the then noted consultants, Howard Marsh and A. E. Comberbatch.

Somehow W. G. Grace managed to maintain his family residence, his medical studies and his cricketing exploits in extraordinary balance. In 1875 Nottinghamshire wrested back the championship for the seventh time since 1864, the year conventionally acknowledged as the commencement of the series. On the sticky softness of the wickets during that damp, humid summer, the masterly batting of Richard Daft and the consistent bowling of Alfred Shaw proved crucial. Grace had a poorish year with the bat, assessed by his own exacting criteria. He certainly played enough, with doubtless the pressure of metropolitan life making it necessary for him to accept a great deal of exhibition cricket. He played no less than 125 innings, 50 of them first-class, and scored some 4,600 runs. His average was down in the 30s, and he scored only three first-class centuries. He managed another four three-figure scores in the second grade, including 210 for the United South versus XVIII of Hastings. Fred Grace played the Gloucester innings of the season when he was undefeated for 180 against Surrey at Clifton.

But if W. G. Grace's batting was below his expected standard, 1875 proved to be his most successful year as a bowler. He took 195 first-class wickets at an average around 12, and thereby accomplished another of his eight 'doubles' of a hundred wickets and over a thousand runs. This was his best year of his best bowling decade, standing out from the years immediately fore and aft only by virtue of the greatest haul of wickets he captured. The 1870s dawned with the advent of the heavy roller and improved groundsmanship. Earlier Grace had depended on his briskly hurrying medium-paced bowling, the straightforward punch and accuracy of which, allied to the vagaries of the pitches, had brought him much joy and success. But W.G. was now a weighty man. He took size fourteen in boots, and it was rumoured that a young bootboy could place his arm up to the elbow inside one of them. Pounding up and down on such huge feet with 15 stone above them was becoming much too laborious for him.

Nothing demonstrates W.G.'s cricketing perspicacity more clearly than the adaptation of his bowling to meet the novel conditions. He recalled the wily craft of William Clarke, his boyhood hero and, in many ways, technical and tactical, his cricket model. In that sense his change of style was the restoration of an older approach, but, after an era of pace, it came as a revelation to his contemporaries. He perfected a slower delivery (his 'bread and butter trick'), high and flighted, which dropped on or near leg stump, with a tendency to drift across the wicket. A superb tactician, he redisposed the orthodox fields of the time, especially strengthening the leg-side. His brother Fred and, as often as not, his cousin W. R. Gilbert would station themselves at deep long-leg while, in addition, W.G. located an extra mid-on, some ten yards behind the wicket. Catches galore were taken in these positions, and the fortification of the on-side was made possible by the bowler's own fielding on the off. He moved swiftly to his left as he bowled, covering many drives in the mid-off and almost into the extra-cover area with magnificent anticipation. Few bowlers have taken as many 'caught and bowled' as W. G. Grace; it is chastening to think that had he been a failure as a batsman, he would have been remembered as the man who took more wickets than anyone else in the nineteenth century.

He was certainly feared as a bowler in the evolving county championship: he had, for instance, taken eighty-four wickets against Yorkshire alone over that first quinquennium of Gloucester cricket. Gloucestershire was destined for two more stirring seasons in a county competition which had become more or less stabilised at this time. The first-class category was known as 'the octarchy' made up of the heavily professionalised sides of the north—Yorkshire, Lancashire and Nottinghamshire; the home counties quartet, much more reliant on amateurs—Kent and its neighbour Sussex, Middlesex and Surrey; and, very much a lone outlying and totally amateur combine, Gloucestershire. This eightsome were to keep exclusive company until the 1890s, when Somerset's brilliance forced the élite to accept them. Derbyshire had had a fitful history but eventually in 1895 became recognised as first-class, while Warwickshire, Essex, Leicester and Hampshire also joined that élite group. Worcester (1899) and Northants (1905) with Glamorgan (1921—the sole post-1914 combatant) completed today's seemingly immovable seventeen.

Like Gloucestershire, almost all the counties had administrative problems from time to time. Composed almost entirely of professionals, Nottinghamshire won or shared the title ten times between 1873 and 1889 but have won it only twice since, in 1907 and 1929. But they suffered most grievously from labour disputes, despite, perhaps because of, their wealth of talent from which other counties, clubs and schools recruited hundreds of coaches and professionals. Following the disturbances of the 1860s, there was also in 1881 a strike of five well-known players, including Shaw and Arthur Shrewsbury, who refused to sign their contracts unless engaged for all matches. It is said the strikers were irritated and unsettled by the financial rewards earned by the Australian visitors of the previous year. Nottinghamshire recovered to take six titles (two shared) in the rest of the decade, but they never thereafter developed the mixture of professional and amateur virtues of which the future county pacemakers were to be formed.

Many county clubs experienced vicissitudes before eventual settlement. According to *Wisden* only four first-class clubs—Derbyshire, Lancashire, Middlesex and Surrey—have the same date for 'first known county organisation' and 'present club'. Six have also had substantial re-organisation of the 'present club'. Taking that into account, the concrete existence of the seventeen first-class counties stems from Surrey (1845) and Sussex (1857) and ends with Yorkshire's reorganisation in 1891, the other fourteen's seminal dates ranging from 1863 to 1888, with no less than eight falling in the 1870s when Gloucestershire were such a power. These were not the only county clubs, as the constant arguments over first-, second- and even third-class status testify. *Wisden* records the dates of formation of twenty-three other English county clubs, although Herefordshire was finally disbanded in 1955, and Westmorland hardly got under way. This means that, amazingly, all forty English counties, as conventionally regarded before the re-organisation of 1972, have had and almost all still have a county club. Their 'first-known' dates stretch from 1787 (Oxfordshire) and 1813 (Cornwall) to 1871 (Cumberland). Their 'present club' dates range from 1871 (Staffordshire, and the only one to stay the same course without reorganisation) to a quartet of post-World War II reformations. But the bulk of the endeavour was pre-1914.

This massive assimilation of cricket into practically every county during the nineteenth century must be unprecedented. No other major sport used the county structure so convincingly at its premier level. When, in 1888, the county borders were mildly reorganised, principally by the establishment of the London County Council, it was decided to ignore the changes for cricketing purposes. When the much less organic and moderate alteration of 1972 brought wholesale changes, the cricket authorities stood firm once more. The cricket authorities are perhaps saner than some realise, for the historic roots of the counties are deep and firm. The English counties command affectionate loyalty, and this is no mere sentiment. For many years they acted as the military and commercial as well as the social and administrative, nexus for English provincial life, and the 1888 Local Government Act, apart from making boundary changes, reinforced that fact with the allocation of a precise series of governmental functions for each county.

For centuries a complex pattern of county cultures, customs and institutions like the judiciary had been developing into what the historian Lewis Namier was perceptively to term the 'county commonwealths' of England. People often lived their entire lives within a shire ambit and their size, shape and numbers seemed admirably adjusted to a nice sense of popular identity. In the seventeenth century well-educated folk would speak of their 'country' when they meant

Cumberland or Wiltshire. Even at the end of the nineteenth century there was still maintained what Professor A. M. Everitt has described as 'the matrix of local society in which political opinion in the provinces was formed'. P. F. Thomas, the cricket historian, has pointed out that many counties were originally kingdoms, and he quotes the splendid text: 'The county spirit enlarges a man out of his own narrow waistband and makes him less of a self-pivoted prig.'

In practical terms, the intricate network of family liaison, popular devotion and administrative know-how made the county the automatic base for high-class cricket at this time. The model was long-established, the interest of the upper social echelons remained and grew, and the complicated and expensive technology of cricket demanded a heavy layout of investment and maintenance. In these ways cricket differed from its competitor for public affection as a team sport, football. The football team had not, in comparative terms, a lengthy history, and football was approximately a hundred years behind cricket in the process of becoming a well-rounded and organised sport. Significantly, professionalism only affected soccer from the 1870s onwards. This meant that in the last quarter of the century, when urban mass spectatorship developed, football was just becoming a highly professionalised sport, in contrast to cricket where the amateur and the county were allied in a powerful revival of both their fortunes.

This had an important corollary. The professional organisation of football became inextricably linked with commerce. This is not to suggest that football clubs were sinful and cricket clubs saintly. County clubs had to make money just as keenly as football clubs. The difference lay in the more literal use of the term 'club' in the world of cricket. The county clubs remained the province of subscribing members, while the football clubs became limited companies, with shareholders and boards of directors.

In the fullness of time it became apparent that where popular support could maintain seventeen first-class cricket clubs and then often only with the liberal donations of wealthy members, there was scope for approaching a hundred Football League clubs, although, again, many of these owed much to local benefactors. A simple yard-stick is that of livelihood: by the end of the century full-time professional footballers outnumbered their cricket counterparts by ten to one.

In brief, whereas the town could sustain a top-grade football team, a parallel cricket team required a county. Professional football was intrinsically an urban game, emerging around the zealous support of workmen enjoying a weekly respite from the rigours of industrial employment. Vicariously, they experienced the fortunes of their favourites in holy communion with thousands of their fellows. Soon there appeared the symbolic artefact of the industrial town: the stands and terraces of the football ground, rising, like a rather seedy and decrepit temple, from the close-packed rows of artisan housing.

Football was substantially moulded by industrialism. Its content was avowedly upper-class, as the early winners of the FA Cup betoken, but it was increasingly handed down to the lower classes. Church, school and university had been, as in cricket, to the fore, but there was also a characteristic element which never influenced first-class cricket. This was the overtly industrial formation. Just as factories, mills and mines ran brass bands, so did they start soccer teams. Of course, they also started cricket teams, but never of any high merit, whereas Manchester United (Newton Heath Loco) and Stoke City (North Staffordshire Railways) began life as industrial clubs.

In football's early days the amateurs played against, but rarely with, the professionals. A few individuals aside, the social integration of the county cricket and indeed the village cricket team was missing from football, and, as professionalism flourished, the top-class amateur footballer just about vanished. The huge difference in time-scale— ninety crowded footballing minutes on a Saturday afternoon as against thirty-six hours spread over six days a week—was also critical. It affected not only the potential audience but also the potential participants. Cricket remained a more complex and more expensive sport. It remained more spacious and lordly, never quite neglecting its rural nor its metropolitan origins.

Such was the fabric and character of first-class cricket as Grace led the glorious Gloucestershire regiment victoriously into battle. In 1876 he led the team to another championship title and, while so doing, produced a superlative series of batting performances. He was in his second year at St Bartholomew's and, almost two years to the day after the birth of his eldest son, another baby boy arrived in July. This was Henry Edgar and he, like his brother, was born a Londoner. Neither medical nor domestic excitements were to distract W.G. from leading Gloucestershire to success, and this was the last time that what was called a purely amateur team was to take the title. The county won five and drew the remaining three of its fixtures, and it was the unbelievable run of scores by their captain which made them invincible.

It is difficult to decide whether the overall statistics or some of the phenomenal specific figures were and are the more shattering to the conventional observer. In about as many innings—118, itself a test of endurance—as in 1875, he almost doubled his average to just above 60. He scored no less than 6,510 runs in all cricket, and 2,622 in first-class cricket. This was his second double thousand, nor, until William Gunn and A. E. Stoddart in 1893, was anyone else to reach an aggregate of 2,000. He scored seven centuries, his regular drubbing of the Players providing one of these. He established what was then a record for any kind of cricket by scoring 400 not out for the United South against XXII of Grimsby. This included 158 singles and the overall total was 681. It took him thirteen and a half hours to penetrate this screen of twenty-two fielders and race out those 400 runs.

At Hull he landed the ball—perhaps the start of all those creaking jokes—on a railway train, as he scored 126 for the United South against the United North, and his colleagues managed only 28 more. But nothing, however startling, could outshine the events of a week or so in the August of 1876. He found himself batting for MCC against Kent at Canterbury on the afternoon of Friday 11 August. It was the second innings, and there seemed little to play for. W.G. hurried the score along, and, by close of play, he was 133 not out. Resuming on the Saturday, he scored a glorious 211 more. His score of 344 was the first-ever triple century in first-class cricket. It beat by 66 the previous highest score, by William Ward all of fifty-six years ago.

On Sunday 13 August, he journeyed up to London, crossed to Paddington and took a train which, Sabbath-wise, ambled down to Bristol. On Monday he scored a sprightly 177 against the extremely strong Nottinghamshire attack at Clifton. His two brothers were in good form—the family provided 304 of Gloucester's 419 total—and a jaded Notts collapsed. On Tuesday and Wednesday, Grace did not bat: he was busy enough, of course, with the ball, polishing off the Nottingham second innings with eight for 69.

The story goes that, changing trains at Birmingham, the dispirited Nottingham XI met a jaunty Yorkshire XI. The latter were on their way to Bristol and, in the way of cricketers, they teased the gloomy Nottinghamshire players without thought either of mercy or the morrow. Yorkshire lost the toss and the 'big 'un', as many of the professionals called him, proceeded to demonstrate that his form and stamina were equally unrelenting. Over eight hours, all day Thursday and during the opening session of Friday, he batted, totalling 216 on

the first and adding another 102 on the second day before Tom
Emmett removed him with what he mysteriously called a
'sostenuster'.

W.G.'s 318 was the highest score in the county championship—it
was indeed the first 300 in that competition, and was both the second
triple century in history and the second in a week. It was to remain the
record for county matches until 1895, when Archie MacLaren destroyed the Somerset attack with a pyrotechnic display of 424. The
Yorkshire bowling of 1876 was superior to Somerset's of 1895, but it
is unlikely that Yorkshire bowlers have ever been so demoralised. It
was described as 'the finest innings ever played by the champion
cricketer'. Some of the Yorkshire professionals refused to bowl. One
or two attempted the stratagem of bowling deliberate wides.

In eight days W.G. had amassed 839 for an average of 419·5. He
had batted, and scored a hundred runs, on each of five days, and, in his
only ten first-class innings of August, he totalled 1,278 runs, surely
the most intensely concentrated thousand runs ever collected in
cricket's history. He had batted seventeen and a half hours during
those eight days and it is said he gave only two chances. His tireless
batting brought him two 7s, four 6s and four 5s and 103 4s. Kent
recruited ten, Notts seven and Yorks eight bowlers.

*The Saturday Review* reckoned, with good reason, that Grace was
'wholly indifferent to atmospheric influences' and that he could
'travel all night and play cricket all day without fatigue or discom-
fort'. The journalist was led in his ecstasy over W.G.'s adventures
toward a 'desire to stop some undersized foreigner and convince him
that Englishmen are the pride and salt of the earth'. Nonetheless, and
without going to the same extremes of patriotism, it is not possible to
read of these exploits without a gasp or two of amazement and
admiration. Grace was at the height of his powers and the zenith of his
achievement. That week encapsulated all that was superb in his
character and skill. No sportsman before, perhaps not since, has, in
eight days, proved himself so absolutely the pre-eminent of his craft.

# 6

# Doctor Grace and the First Australians (1877/8)

The maternal 'Willie' had long since become the more heartily masculine 'Gilly' for those privileged, as when answering a call for a run, to address W.G. in the familiar form. And Gilly, for all his triumphs, was, technically, a slightly ageing medical student with a wife and two babies, attempting to live in London. But with another successful season with the United South XI behind him and his advantage as a drawcard nearing its peak, he seemed able to cope. He buckled down to his second autumn and winter at Bart's and thus was not available for, had he even been inclined to join, James Lillywhite's 1876/7 tour of Australia. In fact this was the first of several all-professional trips to the Antipodes, and, in that the pundits are prepared to accept the first-ever Test match as occurring in the January of that tour, there began a series of several Tests in Australia, with England captained by a professional. Arthur Shrewsbury and Alfred Shaw were the chief cases in point.

Over in Australia Billy Midwinter had progressed to inter-state or, as it was then called, inter-colonial cricket, performing passably well as an all-rounder for Victoria in nine games against the other colony, New South Wales. He was known as the 'Sandhurst Infant' or the 'Bendigo Giant'. Midwinter was chosen for that Australia-England match, becoming—if the designation 'Test' is allowed—not only one of the first-ever 'Test' cricketers, but the first English-born cricketer to play for Australia. He acquitted himself well, not so much in batting as in bowling. Of Australia's first innings of 245 he managed only 5—this was the innings to which Bannerman contributed the first ever 'Test' century, a magnificent 165. Midwinter scored 17—

the top score was 20—out of 104 at the second attempt. With the ball he helped destroy the English, taking five for 28 in their first innings of 196. He took only one second-innings wicket at a cost of 22 (match figures of six for 50) but he played his part well. He bowled no less than 76 balls for those few runs, keeping a tidy end whilst Kendall devastated the England batting with seven for 55. England were all out for 108 and lost by 45 runs.

A month previously he had scored 41 against the tourists in a low scoring 'colonial' match by what the Melbourne press called 'brilliant cricket' and including three 5s. In the return 'Test', which England won, he scored 31 and 12 and took two for 55 on aggregate, another reasonable performance. More than that, his figures in the Australian averages for that season were sturdy enough. Playing for Melbourne and Victoria, he had a batting average of over 18, with 184 runs in ten innings—Horan topped the averages with 40. In his ten first-class matches he also bowled over 1,300 balls for only 401 runs scored against him, taking 32 wickets for an average just a little over 12.

It was the success of this season, particularly against the English tourists, which convinced him that he should try his luck at home. Perhaps Grace, recalling his promise and hearing of his progress, had remained in touch, or resumed contact, possibly through one of the tourists. He may have made some move himself. Competent as his performances had been, he would not have been first choice among the Australians if Grace or anyone had been able to choose. In other words, he must somehow have indicated his availability, although none of Gloucester's amateurs were in the 1876/7 touring squad. However, it is interesting to read the assessment then of 'Mid' in Conway's *Australian Cricketer's Annual*:

> enjoys the reputation of being the hardest hitter in Australia. It seems a pity he does not oftener use his immense strength and reach for offensive work. He plays steadily at times, but that style of play does not suit him, as he is very stiff and cramped: he, however, has a good defence. His hitting against the All-England XI will long be remembered by those who witnessed it. He is a good medium-paced bowler with a high delivery, having a fair command of the ball and a slight breakback. He is a good, but not brilliant, field. Left for England at the end of last season to try his skill in the old country. He is a native of Gloucestershire.

The 'hitting' was the spectacular 41 with its three 5s. 'Mid' certainly was of the requisite size for a slogger. He was a twenty-six-year-old

athlete, 6 foot 2½ inches tall and weighing 14 stone. He was also a
billiards player, a crack shot and a quarter-miler. He was tantamount
to being the model of the 'Bondi democrat', hugely fit and excelling at
several sports.

He arrived in London in May 1877, after his second transoceanic
trip of some weeks. The *Melbourne Standard* and *Cricket* in 1891
both recorded his salty anecdote of his re-introduction to England.
His travelling companion was one Denmark Jack, and both were
unpolished and unsophisticated products of the Bendigo sub-culture.
'Mid' realised that the North was playing the South at the Oval and so
'chartered a cab' to transport them thither. He assumed the journey
from London Docks was much the same as that from the Queen's
Wharf, Melbourne to that city's cricket ground. Such was the distance covered that William 'came to the conclusion that the cabby
was simply driving them about to see the sights of London out of sheer
philanthropy'. Then the cab-driver charged them 10s.6d. Much as he
liked the cab and much as he wished to own a horse, William confessed 'he had no desire to buy the whole concern'. When the cab-
owner mentioned the police, Denmark Jack had second thoughts for
he had 'vague recollections of being to a police station before'. They
paid and went to the match. After the day's play, they enjoyed what
'Mid' termed 'a real good tuck-in'. It cost them 7s.6d apiece, once
more to their surprise and annoyance. William told the waiter that, in
Australia, 7s.6d would pay for a week's board and 15s would buy a
man 'his own eating house'. The waiter followed them to the door, as
if thinking, as Denmark Jack put it, 'that they'd collared his spoons'.
'Remember the waiter', he begged. 'Remember the waiter',
expostulated Midwinter, bursting with astonishment. He spoke
severely to him 'We're not likely to forget you, I assure you.' The
waiter told them humbly that he received no wages. 'Mid' gave him a
sixpence and told him to go to Australia where a man was paid for his
work 'without having to beg for his wages'.

Having arrived in England with only 30s., William Midwinter was
practically bankrupt inside twenty-four hours. In that same day he had
demonstrated many colonial traits—contempt for the customs of a
'foreign' land, a little nostalgia for and pride in the one left behind, the
errors of the naive and provincial, and amazement at metropolitan
prices. Besides all this, it is typical of his enthusiasm that he went
straight from the boat to the cricket. And doubtless he made an early
contact with W. G. Grace, playing at the Oval for the South, for he
was immediately drafted into Grace's 'circus' team, the United South

of England XI. He played at Birmingham, Holbeck and Barrow-in-Furness, in the then usual preface to the county season.

Then at that point William Midwinter established another 'first'. He was signed on by Grace as Gloucestershire's first-ever regular professional, though one called Hall had played a match or two. It is typical of the view of the professional that Midwinter should have been regarded by Gloucester as a mainline bowler who batted, whereas in Australia he was treated more as a batsman who bowled. Thus he entered into a close relationship with W. G. Grace. For six seasons they opened the bowling for Gloucestershire. W.G. also worked hard on W.E.'s batting. As *Cricket* recorded, Grace 'had taken him in hand and he completely altered his batting'. What this meant was that he gave him a stricter balance of the offensive and defensive. This, again, was an essential part of the professional's task. There were matches to be saved and ends to be kept up, especially when one of the Graces was going well at the other. So, instead of his mix of hesitance and harum-scarum onslaughts, Grace introduced an orderly and deliberate element.

Certainly 'Mid' justified the faith in his bowling during his first match for the county. It was the Champion county versus England at the Oval. Although he scored only 1 and did not bat a second time, he had the glorious figures of seven for 35 and four for 46 (match figures, eleven for 81) as Gloucester beat England by five wickets in a low-scoring affair. In the first innings Grace took the outstanding three wickets for 37. The two bowled unchanged, dismissing a useful England side for 83. It was a spectacular beginning to a long partnership.

This was a time when few county matches were played. The England game opened the county's first-class fixtures at the end of June, and, in fact, Gloucestershire's six county matches were all completed in August, save for the last Saturday in July. Gloucestershire won five and drew one and thus retained the championship, albeit for the last time in the county's history so far. The draw was slightly in their favour as well, with Yorkshire, at Sheffield, 121 for nine, still 20-odd runs behind. The wins were against Surrey, Sussex, the home game against Yorkshire, and a double over Nottinghamshire. There were no fixtures with the other three members of the 'octarchy'.

As for 'Mid', he scored 183 runs in the first-class games, with his average of just over 26 putting him fourth in the list behind the three Graces, and with his top score a stolid 68 against Yorkshire cast in his

new obdurate image and a collection of £15 to boot. He took 28
wickets for 364 runs (average exactly 13). Apart from his derring-do
at the Oval, his best bowling was in the last match, against Surrey at
Clifton College, when he took three for 29 and five for 25. In the
previous match, against Sussex the same week at Clifton, he had
match figures of seven for 57. Arguably, he had three good games,
taking only two wickets in the other four matches. However he could
well have been proud of his 0 for 17 in 22 overs against Yorkshire,
while Grace was plundering plenty of wickets at the opposite end.
W.G. took seventeen for 89—his best-ever bowling analysis—in the
Nottinghamshire match at Cheltenham, after which Gloucester
played a local XI and scored 299 with broomsticks, E. M. Grace
topping a hundred and 'Mid' getting a half century.

On 17 July he had made his first appearance (and the first appearance of an Australian-reared cricketer) at Lord's, for a combined
Gloucestershire and Yorkshire team against the Rest of England; at
the time it was written 'He was a fine hard-hitting batsman, but
steady; an effective middle-pace, round-armed bowler, with considerable spin, and an excellent field, generally at a distance from the
wicket.' All in all, it was a commendable and profitable season, and he
stayed on in England, living among his kinsfolk, for the winter. Well-
to-do by their standards, he—like most other professionals—was
quite content to enjoy the luxury of living in simple indolence while
the less fortunate worked.

Grace was hugely pleased with his capture, not least because the
bowling onus was lifted somewhat from his shoulders. Both over 6
feet, and sharing nearly 30 stones between them, they must have been
an intimidating sight, although neither bowled at high pace. W.G.'s
own performances were, as ever, at the heart of Gloucestershire's
most successful season. 1877 was another 'double' season for him,
with 1,474 first-class runs for an average of 39, and 179 wickets. His
batting was less potent than in the summer of 1876, but, in fairness, it
should be added that Lockwood was the only other player to reach a
thousand runs and W.G. topped the averages. Once again, moreover,
his bowling more than compensated for any mild cavilling disappointment in his batting. Most vividly, he took the last seven Nottingham
wickets in his record-breaking bowling stint without a run being
scored off him, with W. R. Gilbert and his brother Fred prowling the
leg boundary and swallowing catch after catch. He had seven centuries: four first-class, two against odds for the United South, and 261
for South against North. He had led his team undefeated through two

seasons, and had guided them to victory over the Rest of England. As
an astute tactician, as well as a supreme all-rounder, was his great
reputation created.

His brothers were his loyal lieutenants. E. M. Grace, 'the little
doctor', with his Dundreary whiskers and red-spotted shirt, actually
topped the county averages. His 'most wonderful' innings ever was
said to be his 89 against Nottinghamshire when the going was rough.
'Keep your eye on Morley, and play carefully, Ted' were the
skipper's instructions. W.G. reported his elder brother's answer as
follows: 'All very well to talk; I should like to know what good the
steadiness of your fellows has done for the innings. It looks to me like a
clear case of funk, and I am going to stop it.' The modern mind may
suspect the authenticity of such an oracular reply at that point in a
cricket match, but the action was assuredly suited to the word, and
Morley was summarily dispatched for several boundaries via E.M.'s
ungracious cross-bat. It was, sadly, Gloucestershire's last title.

While Billy Midwinter relaxed into his first English winter since
childhood, his county skipper was moving his family again although
he first, in September 1877, suffered the fright of being shot near the
eye while indulging in that risky sport at Apethorpe. Luckily for W.G.
and thousands of spectators, it turned out to be only a superficial
wound.

W.G. had now completed two and a half years at Bart's, their even
tenor frequently and irregularly disturbed by two seasons of the fullest
cricket programmes the Champion ever negotiated. There still
remained a further heavily theoretical backlog to complete, as well as a
final practical session. With the former largely in mind, and probably
with the family finances not too far from his thoughts, he moved back
to Gloucestershire. The Graces set up house with Henry, the oldest of
the brothers, now in his forties, at Kingswood Hill, and W.G. tried to
master the mysteries of medical science. Henry, an affable and prosperous general practitioner welcomed them to 'The Cottage', his
home throughout his entire professional life, and it was useful to have
an amateur tutor on hand.

By late autumn it was clear that Agnes was pregnant once more. In
May 1878, just as the cricket season was in early bloom, Bessie was
born, W.G.'s only daughter and without doubt his favourite child.
The protracted studies and a third child on the way concentrated his
thoughts intensely. This was the winter when Grace came close to
putting the temptations of cricket behind him. He reasoned that his
growing family needed the support of a well-qualified and busy

professional man. It has often been said that the arrival of the first Australians shook W.G. out of this mundane torpor, and, like the fire-horse pawing the ground and lifting its head at the clamour of the alarm bell, he took down his bat, oiled it and practised assiduously for the fray.

It is true Grace was no lover of his overseas adversaries in general, much as he befriended one or two of them as individuals, and John Conway, the Australian manager, was his especial bête noir. He took the Antipodean invasion very seriously indeed. At the same time, one should never underestimate the single-mindedness with which Grace approached cricket, the manner in which he had been drilled in its values since infancy, and his obsessional drive to triumph over and again. It would have been all but unbearable for Grace, England's leading sporting idol at the height of his career, to have yielded to the call of domesticity. Perhaps the Australians were the excuse he required to shrug off the cobwebs of caution. Then there was the commercial angle: £1,500 is said to have been his fee for the 1873/4 Australian tour, at present (1980) values that was worth something like £18,000—not bad for a medical student on honeymoon! By 1879, because of Grace's virtuosity, the United South XI had driven off the competition of most of the other exhibition XIs and W.G.'s combine more or less monopolised an admittedly narrower field. Take for example, 1873, when the USEE played fifteen matches, winning five, losing seven and drawing three. The itinerary was: 12 May, Oxford XXII; 22 May, Edinburgh XVIII; 29 May, Darlington XVIII; 16 June, Alexandra Park (Manchester) XXII; 19 June, Broughton XVIII; 7 July, Leicester XXII; 10 July, Wakefield XXII; 11 August, Coventry XII; 18 August, East Hants XXII; 4 September, Lincoln XXII; 8 September, Inverness XXII; 11 September, Aberdeen XXII; 15 September, Northampton XXII; 18 September, Leinster XXII; and 22 September, New Cross Albion XXII. These fixtures, all against odds, were dovetailed with the first-class programme. There was an early series in May, before the county and other major games were properly underway, a week engineered in each of the high summer months and that final, madcap September scramble, involving trips to the Highlands and across the Irish Sea, before the reality of autumn was grudgingly recognised. Grace himself scored 825 runs for an average of 27, and the fact that he had thirty-one innings in fifteen games reminds one that supplementary exhibitions had to be organised if games collapsed too early. Grace also took 91 wickets for 574 runs, an average of about 9.

More interesting than the cricketing is the financial data. What did

Grace, organiser and secretary, make out of this? Apart from W. R. Gilbert and Fred Grace, the other players listed for this season were all professionals, and they were all paid £5 a game and it is known that both those amateurs did receive payments. Most of these games were played before what Lillywhite's almanac for several of them described as a 'large assemblage' and, occasionally, as the biggest crowd ever gathered to watch cricket in the given district. Grace was a tremendous draw, and it is obvious that several thousands would often be present, paying probably a shilling or maybe sixpence a head. The local lessees were chiefly interested in the catering and bar concessions, and, apart from travel and board, the overheads were not excessive. Although it is difficult to calculate with much precision, it is possible that a tour of that description produced a net profit of as much as £2,000.

The problems were twofold. There was the sportsman's usual anxiety about the effect of age on career and there was, for Grace, the additional social issue of being, in modern argot, a shamateur. The hypocrisy was not at all pronounced: no one pretended that Grace was not profiting from the United South's enterprises. The fact that he organised it, rather than just played for it, possibly helped, in that it suggested the Victorian businessman and not the paid artisan. It was, nevertheless, an inconsistent and sometimes uncomfortable situation, but it enabled the Graces, financially, to cope.

In fact, 1878 was something of a compromise, for Grace played rather less second-grade cricket. Living at Kingswood Hill, and away from the metropolis, was an aid in resisting too many calls to arms, while, obviously enough, his medical studies were more simply fitted into a cricket schedule than his more rigidly timetabled studentship at Bart's. But it was not the best of W.G.'s seasons. He barely topped the thousand (1,115 runs for an average of 29, his lowest for some years) and scored only one century (116 in the county match against Nottinghamshire). However, Ulyett, the Yorkshire professional, was the only other player to reach a thousand runs in a summer of mixed weather, and Grace did achieve yet another double with a bag of 148 wickets at 14 runs apiece. But, a sad omen, England this time beat Gloucester by six wickets and the county failed to come near to retaining the championship.

During that chilly summer David Gregory captained the twelve Australians who struggled to handle a daunting programme of thirty-seven fixtures, half of them against odds. It was a profit-sharing tour, preceded by a money-raising set of domestic fixtures. This gave rise to much acrimony: several professionals, for instance, refused to play against them for the Players at the Oval because of a row over the niggardly terms the Australians offered.

Although there was no game styled as an international, the MCC fielded a strong side including W. G. Grace, A. N. Hornby, Alfred Shaw, Morley and G. G. Hearne. It was 27 May and a famous and historic day, when, as *Punch* had it, 'The Australians came down like a wolf on the fold.' Spofforth proved excessively lupine. He took ten for 20 (including a hat-trick) in the match, and 'Mid's' old pal, Harry Boyle, had six for 3 in the second innings. It was the Australians' first visit to Lord's, and the match lasted no more than a day. MCC were contemptuously dismissed for 33 and 19, and although their gloating opponents scored only 41 at the opening attempt, they were left with a mere dozen runs for victory and won by nine wickets. W.G. scored 4 and 0. In the second innings he was clean bowled by Spofforth, who on that arduous tour had, unbelievably, 326 victims. As *Punch* continued, in one of the most celebrated of its puns, 'Grace after dinner did not get a run.' As for Billy Midwinter, he scored 10, and, as thirty-one wickets fell for 105 runs, he emerged as the only player to reach double-figures. It was another of his peculiar 'firsts', for he thus became the first Australian batsman to reach double figures at Lord's.

In 1878 occurred the most dramatic incident of 'Mid's' career. Eleven Australians had arrived with a view to Midwinter joining their company. At that time the actual county season started very late and the Australians played their first match on 20 May. 'Mid' had already, in fact, played for the United South of England and two England XIs prior to this, and he then commenced a string of nine games with the tourists, including the MCC fixture. He was the phlegmatic mercenary plying his craft wherever it paid best, but, in what was still a confused situation over fixture lists and eligibility, Midwinter got entrapped into a confrontation. *Cricket*, for instance, was quite clear that he was 'drafted into the team of 1878 and not chosen'. In other words, he had not been formally selected in Australia and an assumption had been made that he would help out. It is reasonably likely that Midwinter might have expected that Gloucestershire—with only thirteen county fixtures in 1878—would have easily reached some compromise with the Australian management, always considering how many teams people like Grace and several of the professionals served. He had perhaps reckoned without the vestiges of bad feeling from the 'honeymoon' tour of Australia, soon exacerbated by Australian accusations of heavy payments to Grace, to his brother G.F., and to their cousin W. R. Gilbert as what the Australian press termed 'so-called Gentlemen cricketers'. Spofforth was in particularly belligerent mood. 'Others may be petrified by W.G.', he defiantly announced, 'but not me.' For his part Grace was 'loath to see him inseparably attached to the Australian team' and, in his memoirs, he claims that Midwinter had 'promised to play for Gloucestershire in all out matches'. One can imagine too how Grace must have been smarting from the wounds of 27 May.

There was little hope of accommodation in such an atmosphere. On 20 June, 'Mid' sat padded up at Lord's, waiting to open the batting with Bannerman. The Coroner, E. M. Grace, and Bush, the huge Gloucester wicket-keeper, flanked the Champion as he strode into Lord's and literally hijacked 'Mid' from under the nose of David Gregory. They talked him into joining them, pads and all, in their waiting cab, which then transported them to the Oval, where Grace had been furious to find his county a man short. Thus was effected what *Cricket* called Midwinter's 'severance from the colonial players'.

John Conway, the Australian manager, organised a group of vigilantes to recapture 'Mid'. David Gregory accompanied the posse, as did 'Mid's' boyhood friend, Harry Boyle. They just managed to overtake the renegade at the Oval gates, and, to the delight of the crowd, a furore took place in which, among other epithets, Grace condemned his opponents as 'a damned lot of sneaks'. He claimed they had caused Midwinter to break his engagement by promise of higher pay.

The debate continued by correspondence. Midwinter played for Gloucester, and the Aussies regarded his 'defection' as a dreadful betrayal. Moreover, until Grace apologised for having 'insulted the whole of the Australian eleven in the most unmistakeable language', the fixture with the Gloucester club would be cancelled. Grace was pleased to have the opportunity of stating that he had not insulted the entire Australian outfit: all his oratorical abuse had been heaped on the head of John Conway, but the Australians were not won over by this defence. The county pointed out that the Australians' actions went far 'to palliate Mr Grace's stormy language'. They knew Midwinter was a Gloucestershire player, and that, apart from playing for the 1877 season, he had already played at Bedminster for the county colts. His engagement could 'hardly fail to have been known to you' and—a telling point—had been discussed by John Conway and J. A. Bush on 17 and 18 June, only two days before the confrontation. Gregory counter-claimed that Midwinter had asked Conway for a place to be kept open for him, but, of course, that was a somewhat dated agreement of a year before. The Australians climbed down a little, and agreed to overlook the 'defection', the Bush-Conway negotiations probably being a critical argument. At this Grace apologised with what dignity he could muster, regretting that 'in the excitement of the moment I should have made use of unparliamentary language to Mr Conway'. He proffered 'a hearty welcome and a good ground at Clifton', and the Australians took him up on both offers, with Spofforth sweeping aside the county and helping to inflict upon them their first-ever home defeat. The county held the visitors to an honourable draw in the return match, with E. M. Grace scoring 55, but with Spofforth once more accounting for W.G. before he had scored. Grace, always, of course, added whatever meiosis he could to the recital, speaking, in his memoirs, of Midwinter leaving Lord's 'after some persuasion' and of the whole business as no more than 'a curious incident'.

In the event Midwinter (who, given so confused a situation, has perhaps unfairly been accused since of 'duplicity') played for neither side, no doubt to avoid further embarrassment. However, he had severely split a thumb which restricted his cricket that summer. Including the controversial Surrey match (he scored 0 and 4, and took four wickets, so his was not a startling intervention), he played only seven first-class matches. He took sixteen for 288 (average 18) and scored only 121 runs for an average of 11—26 against Nottinghamshire and four for 28 in the same game were his best performances. Yorkshire gave Gloucester a terrible thrashing by 244 runs, with Ulyett and Lockwood both scoring centuries. Incidentally another 'first' accrued to 'Mid' during that foreshortened season. In scoring 16 not out in two and a half hours in the Nottinghamshire match he became the first Australian to carry his bat in first-class cricket.

There were also pleasant and charming affairs to record of the summer of 1878. In July Gloucestershire paid its first visit to Old Trafford, and the attraction of the Graces was such that the entrances could not deal with the crowds: 16,000 were present on the Saturday, and, over the three days, 28,000 witnessed the match. The Saturday receipts were a record £400. The game ended in an even-handed draw, with Gloucestershire, five wickets in hand and Grace at the crease, requiring 111 to win. Midwinter scored 22 and 25 in this low-scoring game. What, of course, is important about this match is that it was immortalised years after by Francis Thompson in the best of cricket's idyllic poems:

It is Glo'ster coming North, the irresistible,
  The Shire of the Graces long ago!
It is Gloucestershire up North the irresistible,
  And new-arisen Lancashire the foe!
A Shire so young that has scarce impressed its traces,
Ah, how shall it stand before all-resistless Graces?
O, little red rose, their bats are as maces
  To beat thee down, this summer long ago!

This day of Seventy-eight they are come up North against thee,
  This day of Seventy-eight, long ago.
The champion of the centuries, he cometh up against thee,
  With his brethren, every one a famous foe!
The long-whiskered Doctor, that laughest rules to scorn,
  While the bowler, pitched against him, bans the day that he was born;
And G.F. with his science makes the fairest length forlorn;
  They are come from the West to work thee woe!

As for the 'long-whiskered Doctor' who 'laughest rules to scorn' it was on 30 August when, according to his biographer, Brownlee, W.G. while batting found the ball lodged in his shirt. It was against Surrey at Clifton. He ran several before a posse of fielders collared him and dragged him to a standstill. He pleaded that had he removed the ball, they might have appealed for 'handled the ball'. After a short conference, three runs were agreed. It was the kind of incident which made the old sweats say that while he might never have broken the rules, it was marvellous what he could do within them.

Back to London went Grace, his academic study more or less complete, for a final year of medical practice, this time at Westminster Hospital. Agnes, her two boys and her baby girl, Bessie, were established in Acton, and the head of the family divided his time between the wards, under the eye of Dr Allchin, and the outpatients department, with Dr de Havilland Hall as his mentor.

The upshot was that it was Whit Monday before Grace made a public appearance in the 1879 season, although he had played a club match or two beforehand. It was Alfred Shaw's benefit and it was ruined by rain. Although Grace's relations with professionals were not always of the friendliest—in part because they perceived themselves as the genuine article—he was punctilious in his aid when they were beneficiaries. Later in the season there was an under-thirties versus over-thirties game which was called a 'complimentary' match, as opposed to 'benefit' match, for Grace's own testimonial. W.G. gave the proceeds to the previously disappointed Shaw. That same year he altered the date of a Gloucestershire fixture to play in Luke Greenwood's benefit at Sheffield. Luke Greenwood had been involved in a famous tale told of Grace's first-ever crushing of the White Rose at Sheffield before a gallery of 23,000. In those days it was sometimes the custom for spectators to return a ball lost or out of the ground personally, often receiving a shilling or sixpence for his or her trouble. During Grace's lashing of the Yorkist attack, an old lady retrieved a far-hit delivery, toddled up to the wicket and presented the ball to the bowler, Luke Greenwood, looking expectantly at him the while. 'Nah', growled that ruffled trundler, 'yon's 'im that 'it it, ye mun go t' 'im for t' brass.' Again when rain ruined the benefit in 1879 of Edgar Willsher, the innovator of legal over-arm bowling, Grace took his own select XI to play Kent by way of compensation. So, in spite of the irritations caused by what A. A. Thomson has called Grace's 'excessive artfulness', he was the soul of generosity when benefits were planned. And if this eased his own conscience at all, then that was a welcome bonus.

The summer of 1879 was, it is contested, the wettest ever. There were scarcely three consecutive fine days from April to September. The rain fell and fell, and, with it, Gloucester's aspirations and standards. With but the one professional, Midwinter, and with the other seven counties possessing a truer balance of gentleman-player strength, Gloucestershire won two and lost three, including, at the hands of Nottinghamshire, its first home defeat by a county. Part of the trouble, in terms both of money and morale, was the lack of public support. Gloucestershire drew very poor crowds. In contrast to the London-based teams and the northern counties, Clifton and Cheltenham enjoyed only sparse attendances, despite the presence of the Champion who, elsewhere, added thousands to many gates. The Cheltenham festival week had been inaugurated the previous year, in 1878, with James Lillywhite, Grace's old antagonist and now coach at the College, stumping up £150 for the county and meeting the local expenses for the concession of managing the week and culling what profit he might. The two school grounds of Clifton and Cheltenham could not, however, pull in the members or the crowds, and Gloucestershire suffered accordingly. This underlines what a *tour de force* old Henry Grace had wrought: he had created a county side where, in reality, there was little potential. Gloucestershire remained the exception proving the rule that a solid population base, both middle and working class, was essential for the Victorian first-class county in the 1870s and 1880s.

The only bright spots were provided by the bowling of W.G. and W. E. Midwinter. Three times they ran through sides—Middlesex for 41 (W.E. two for 25; W.G. six for 16); Lancashire 53 (W.E. three for 12, W.G. seven for 37); and Notts 61 (W.E. four for 23, W.G. six for 37), although Arthur Shrewsbury's excellent 87 in the second innings of that third match led Nottinghamshire to a six-wicket win. Grace also had match figures of fifteen for 116 against Surrey at Clifton, and they shared fifteen wickets at the Oval in the return game. W.G. had three centuries that year, including 123 against Surrey in that same match, when G.F. and he shared 180 out of a total of 239. In all, he took 105 wickets but for once failed to reach a thousand runs. He finished with 880. In Gloucester matches 'Mid' took 41 wickets at 165 each and averaged 20 (total 282) with the bat, with the second of his only two half centuries thus far, both against Yorkshire. In the high-scoring Middlesex fixture, when 1,063 runs were scored for 27 wickets, he soldiered on and obtained five for 106.

Although he had only played a couple of seasons, he was given a benefit game against Lancashire at Clifton, and, unluckily, it rained yet again. The county gave him £100, with the bait of another £100 should he play when required until 1883. He neither received nor earned that second compensation, but 1878 and 1879 serve to demonstrate the vulnerability of the Victorian professional. 'Mid' received £8 a match, a goodly fee for that era. Because of his split thumb he earned only £56 in 1878, whereas the following year he collected £96 for twelve matches, in many of which there was little actual play because of rain.

But however dispiriting a season it had proved, W. G. Grace found in 1879 the perfect recompense, for, in November, his medical studies finally reached a successful climax. He received the diploma installing him as Licentiate of the Royal College of Physicians of Edinburgh and a member of the Royal College of Surgeons. From now on it was Doctor Grace.

# 7
# *Doctor Grace and the Amateur Revival: The Australians* (1879-84)

Henry Grace's most famous son had now fulfilled his dual ambition of sporting prowess and professional status. Perhaps W. G. Grace recalled how diligently his father had served both causes, and how, for instance, he had once sat with a patient for three days and nights until, when relieved, his boots had to be cut from off his feet. Perhaps W.G. remembered also his father's death. Drenched on the Duke of Beaufort's hunt, he had caught an inflammation, insisted on journeying out to see an ailing patient, and had deteriorated and died within a day or so.

It was the future, however, which had to rule Grace's actions. He was a GP without a practice, and a practice cost money. In order to provide him with such support a testimonial fund was launched by the MCC in 1879. There was a testimonial match, as well as other activities and a list for contributors, and the sum raised was £1,458. The Over-Thirties played the Under-Thirties, and, although, unusually for so big an occasion, Grace fell twice for paltry scores of 7 and 0, he took nine wickets for 87 in the match, and his brothers E.M. and G.F. excelled for opposite sides. During this match on 23 July, the presentation was made to Grace of the money, a marble clock and a pair of bronze ornaments. Few could recall an amateur being so treated, while it was too ornate and formalised for any professional. It was, advisably, a testimonial rather than a benefit.

The proceedings took place in front of the Lord's pavilion. Lord FitzHarding, vice-president of Gloucestershire, made the presentation, explaining that the original idea had been to purchase a practice for Mr Grace, as he still formally was. It was decided he 'was old enough to take care of himself' (laughter and cheers), but, obviously, a gift in kind would have looked less tarnished. The compromise was a gentle insistence that 'They would leave him to choose a practice for himself.' Mr Grace—'I am not a speech-maker'—made his by now characteristic 'short and appropriate reply', and ears were bent to Lord Charles Russell, oldest member of the MCC and a member of an even older distinguished family. In his eulogy of Grace he summed up the essence of W.G.'s cricket.

> The game must be played with the head and the heart, and in this respect Mr Grace was eminently prominent. Looking at Mr Grace's playing, I am never able to tell whether that gentleman was playing a winning or a losing game. I have never seen the slightest lukewarmness or inertness in him in the field. If you want to see Mr Grace play cricket, I would ask you to look at him playing one ball. You all know the miserably tame effect of the ball hitting the bat instead of the bat hitting the ball, whether acting on the offensive or the defensive. In playing a ball, Mr Grace puts every muscle into it from the sole of his foot to the crown of his head.

It was a fair commentary.

W. G. Grace bought a practice, as might have been expected, back in the Bristol area, one of four brothers now doctoring a large slice of the land they knew so well to the east of the city. His surgery was at Stapleton Road, Bristol, and, as a tidy and bespoke element in his income, he became the official parish doctor, serving for twenty years those patients covered by the poor law regulations. The Grace's new home was Thrissle Lodge, adjacent to the incumbent's practice, but they soon moved a few yards to Thrissle House, where, true to the family tradition, W.G. prepared 30 square yards of a practice pitch, albeit a somewhat sloping one. Later he moved to Victoria Square, Clifton, where he was conveniently located near the college ground. Later still he moved to Ashley Grange when Ashley Down was developed as the county headquarters from 1887. In 1882 the Grace family was completed with the arrival of Charles Butler, the only one of W.G.'s three sons actually to be born in Gloucestershire. Master Gilbert was now eight and, for a couple of seasons now, he had been busily helping to keep the score on the Clifton ground.

The organisation of the first Grace testimonial by the MCC illustrated the emergence of the Marylebone club from a slough of despond. After the ignominious failure of its 1873 'Silver Cup' competition, the MCC had left it to the counties to resolve their own problems, but, gradually, during the 1880s, the need was felt for some arbiter to evaluate the eligibility of counties and the qualifications of players. County secretaries began to meet annually in 1882 and, with W. G. Grace their grateful and enthusiastic adherent, MCC came more to the fore. In 1884 the club took almost complete responsibility for the great revision of the laws of the game: 21 April was the grand day. That the umpires should be 'absolutely satisfied' with a delivery was inserted in the no-ball law; and boundaries—although operative in many instances hitherto—were mentioned in the laws for the first time. Legal dominion set its seal on the MCC's rule and membership sprang from 650 in the 1860s to over 2,000 by the early 1880s, a seventh of whom were titled. In 1877 Middlesex began to play its matches at Lord's and fine new facilities were added, such as a press box and the mound stand.

In Christopher Brookes's view, in *English Cricket*, the success of W. G. Grace was, at this juncture, crucial: 'in his freedom lay the hope of things to come'. His huge success, sporting and commercial, signalled and personified the amateur revival and the re-possession of the game by the establishment. The schisms and strikes of the 1860s and after had fatally wounded the professional endeavours to control cricket, and the monotony of exhibition XIs forever winning and never developing any popular identity also told its tale.

It was galling for the professionals to realise that W. G. Grace had taken his part in the amateur resuscitation by his promotion of their own invention in his organisation of the United South. But this team, too, with the beginnings of Grace's professional career as a doctor and the enlargement of the first-class programme, followed its coevals into oblivion by 1882. In one of its final games, W.G. scored 122 against XXII of the Mark of Bosworth in the semi-darkness of 12 September. In part-reaction to what were seen as the dangers of over professional-ism, the counties gained apace. The professionals accepted that the county clubs were their natural employers, and, in Brookes's phrase, 'This subtle ''divide and rule'' strategy enabled a deeply conservative institution to withstand the challenge.' There was a resolution of the class gap between 'the aristocratic MCC and the middle-class counties', as represented by men like Henry Grace and his sons, a resolution encouraged by a joint anxiety about overweening profes-sionalism. 'Self has taken a great hold on cricket', said H. Silver, a contemporary cricket writer, in a revealing sentence, 'The average mania is as fatal to cricket as trade unions are to commerce.'

The amateur character of Gloucestershire and its triumphs of the late 1870s were the heartening injection county cricket required.

A. G. Steel of Marlborough, Cambridge University and Lancashire, was one of the most effective all-rounders of all time, and a stream of brilliant batsmen—Alfred Lubbock, A. N. Hornby, I. D. Walker, for instance—poured from the public schools and universities. With the dawn of the 1880s the balance was adjusting, as a noble generation of professional batsmen, Maurice Read, William Gunn, Arthur Shrewsbury, arose. The era of professional and amateur harmony was at hand.

Curiously, the combination of workmanlike professionalism and country-house selectiveness which marked the coming decades of county cricket played Gloucestershire, doyen of amateurism, false. A lack of professional support left them bereft, and they fell dismally away in the county championship as Nottinghamshire, chiefly, along with Surrey and Lancashire, progressed. In 1880 they signed W. A. Woof, another quick bowler, whom Midwinter thereafter referred to, in that engaging way of cricketers with those who might threaten to oust them, as his 'pupil'.

The next five seasons were mixed ones, socially and professionally, for Dr Grace. Gloucester's problems apart, he had to accommodate the daily business of being a doctor. In 1883 he even missed, for the first time since 1867, a Gentlemen and Players match. He had a nasty bout of mumps in 1882 and in 1884 he injured his hand and played some of the season with a bandaged leg. In 1881, for the first time since 1875, W.G. did not top the averages. Significantly, it was that sprightly little amateur, A. N. Hornby, who toppled the maestro. Grace never achieved the double in those years; indeed (with a bare 101 in 1882) he only reached a hundred wickets once, while a thousand runs evaded him except in 1883 and 1884, when he rallied, especially in that latter year, with a fine tally of 1,762 runs. He never, however, led the averages throughout the 1880s.

But compared with ordinary cricketers, W.G.'s doings remained godlike in scope. In these five years he still notched up a couple of dozen centuries, most of them first-class, but including some for the Thornbury club as well as the United South. His 182 at Trent Bridge in 1881 was the highest score of the county season, but the following year he managed no first-class century at all. Still, in 1884 the Players found him on a good day for the umpteenth time and he scored a century against them, while, typically, he seemed to save his best efforts for the Australians. In 1884 he scored three centuries against them on behalf of Gloucestershire, the Gentlemen and the MCC.

The Australian presence was now a regular one. Following

Gregory's tour in 1878, Lord Harris, his happy band of amateurs reinforced by a couple of Yorkshire professionals, had visited Australia. It was an ill-starred trip when (and Grace quoted the alliterative phrase in his memoirs) 'rowdyism became rampant'. *The Australasian* newspaper recorded how, when W. L. Murdoch was adjudged run out at Sydney, there was a near riot. Lord Harris was struck with a whip or stick, and, for his part, he roundly accused his hosts of having 'professional betting men in the pavilion'. His team were defeated by an Australian XI, and this *Wisden* counts as a Test match.

One consequence was a cool reception for Murdoch's tourists to England in the summer of 1880 and they had difficulty in finding reasonable fixtures. They had played only two or three top-class matches, when, right at the end of the season in early September, Lord Harris and the Surrey secretary C. W. Alcock, in desperation, arranged a representative XI to meet them at the Oval. It was an exciting match, played before, it was claimed, the largest crowd ever assembled for a game of cricket. W. G. Grace was on his best form and his best behaviour. He worked steadily for a 'severe and safe' 152. Poor Fred Grace had an embarrassing pair of ducks, but made historic amends by catching Bonnor off what is claimed to be the highest caught hit in cricket's annals. The batsmen scampered three before the ball came to rest, in Fred Grace's secure hands.

Australia were without a crippled Spofforth, and W.G., scoring England's first-ever Test century, laid the foundation for a total of 420. Australia followed on, but, in his turn, Murdoch, the Australian skipper, scored an undefeated 153. England still only needed 57, but lost five wickets for 20 runs, before W.G. and the amateur Frank Penn stopped the rot. 20,000 people watched on each of the first two days of what is now regarded as the first international on English soil.

The see-saw continued. In the winter of 1881 Shrewsbury, Shaw and Lillywhite managed the first of three professional tours of the Antipodes. They played two matches each against 'combined Australia' and 'the Eleven for England', all four games now reckoned as Test matches. That XI for England, again captained by Murdoch, played no less than thirty-eight fixtures from May to the end of September. To guarantee decent crowds, they refused to start before noon or continue after six. During the 1880s there were several internal disputes in Australian cricket, all of them vitiating its strength, all of them caused by arguments over money. Murdoch's team did, however, play one Test, and that a celebrated one. At the Oval in the late rainy August of 1882 Spofforth, in another breathtaking exhibition, took fourteen for 90, his last spell reading four for 2 in 11 overs, as England fell for 77, needing 85. Grace scored a paltry 4 at his first attempt, but managed 32 in the second innings. 'I left six overs', he said angrily, 'to get 32 runs, and they couldn't get 'em.' It was an exciting match. One spectator dropped dead and another gnawed his way through his umbrella handle—and the famous obituary in the *Sporting Times* immortalised the match as the one from which the 'Ashes' stems.

The Hon. Ivo Bligh immediately took a mainly amateur side to Australia in the winter of 1882/3 sharing the honours in four purported Test matches. In 1884 Murdoch arrived for the third time, on this occasion losing one and drawing two Tests, and leaving the mythical 'Ashes' in England. Grace played in all three Tests, and his most surprising contribution was at the Oval when, with Murdoch compiling a pitiless 211—the record Test innings in England for the next forty-six years—he kept wicket. Alfred Lyttelton, removing the gloves, bowled his lobs successfully, and W.G. actually caught Midwinter off one of them. The wicket-keeper ended with four wickets for 19.

These tours were usually commercial enterprises, with the touring parties gaining kudos by labelling themselves with their national title. There may have been other facets, such as the patriotic or the missionary or, for amateurs, something akin to the Grand Tour in the educative experience of an Australian trip. But, as in most forms of Empire-building, commerce was the chief motivator. *Cricket* in its very first edition, of 10 May 1882, had this to say of Australian cricket:

> Indeed, bookmakers seem to be among the chief patrons of the game, as is, perhaps, not unnatural where the line between gentlemen and players is almost non-existent to the naked English eye. The Australians are excellent cricketers . . . but the colony does not possess the class of men from whom the Hornbys, Webbs and Harrises are drawn, the class of gentlemen of leisure who can afford to give the time and trouble to organising the pastime and keeping up its moral and social tone.

The article spoke of two English professionals bribed during the Harris tour of 1878/9. A third refused to be corrupted and disclosed the conspiracy. There were, *Cricket* claimed, very large sums for those 'ready to sell their faith', more than all the bets on English cricket in a year. 'The colonists have that provincial esprit de corps which only cares for the result of the match.'

That rather condescending attitude was also taken towards English professionals desirous of improved conditions. In 1881 occurred the 'Nottinghamshire Schism', when seven Nottinghamshire professionals refused to play until certain contractual items were agreed and they were allowed, as in the past, to organise their own 'exhibition' matches. They were encouraged in this action by the way in which 'the colonial players' had screwed exorbitant demands out of English clubs, but the county committee, supported by the cries of outrage nationwide, stood firm, dropped the players and surrendered the championship to Lancashire. What Lillywhite's *Cricketer's Annual* called 'a deliberate combination' was foiled and thereafter no such collective action was contemplated by the professionals. 'Hence a combination among the labourers', said *Cricketer's Companion* loftily, 'for the purpose of getting higher wages is, we think, improper.'

'We trust', said *Cricket*, 'that the colonial vice will not take firm root' and that 'we play for play's sake not for victory.' One should not be 'overwhelmed with mortification at loss' or 'puffed up with pride' at victory. The professionals, having been momentarily stimulated by the 'pecuniary speculation' of the Australians, collapsed. The 'exhibition' games were over, and, professional tours overseas apart, the counties reigned supreme.

That was all very fine, but how did it square with W. G. Grace and his testimonial fund and his contractual obligations, now ending, with the United South? It must all have rankled bitterly. Gradually amateurs were to find themselves in receipt of payments, for hotel and travelling expenses, sometimes to excess and in compensation for business losses incurred. When Grace settled into his practice, Gloucestershire paid for a locum for him in the summer, and, as time went by, for two such substitutes. It was all very well for Lord Charles Russell to talk, at Grace's presentation in 1879, of the 'national essentials of patience, fortitude and pluck' manifest in cricket, which fostered 'the respect for law, and love of fair play which are characteristic of us English people'. Cricket may, as Lord Charles opined, have appealed to all 'from the prince to the peasant', but its rewards varied according to social status. At this time a young professional would have started at £1 a week, with no winter retainer. A year later, in 1880, at the annual general meeting of the MCC there was a furore concerning 'sums much in excess of actual expenses . . . frequently paid to gentlemen by other clubs and individuals'.

The accusation was directed at other clubs, such as, presumably

Gloucestershire. MCC preferred to view themselves, like Caesar's wife, as above suspicion. The club had also much extended the work they offered professionals, especially in the season's early days, when a troupe of bowlers was employed for practice purposes and as supporting artillery in MCC sides. They would often have to act as assistant groundsmen as well, possibly doing all manner of menial jobs. In 1880, for instance, MCC signed on no less than twenty-seven professionals. One of them was Billy Midwinter, and for this and the next two seasons, he demonstrated yet another angle on the life of the Victorian cricket professional.

That summer he played in all Gloucestershire's eleven first-class games—of which they won four and lost two—including one against Australia in which he had match figures of six for 116. In all he took 54 wickets for 850, his highest haul for the county, and he also scored his first century—103 against Surrey at Cheltenham. Yorkshire were again his favourite team: he took six for 29 as they crashed for 95 at Sheffield.

It was during this summer that a great truth dawned on W. E. Midwinter. For since the sun is always, at least in theory, shining somewhere on our globe, it was possible, if transport were available, to play cricket, and play cricket for money, the whole year round. It was in September 1880, and in a ship, the *Lusitania*, that he became the world's first inter-continental cricketer. He sustained this until he re-settled in Australia in 1882. This meant that he played cricket continuously over half-a-dozen seasons, three in England and three in Australia. He was aboard ship for some twelve of those thirty-six months. It was a formidable enterprise and one of far-reaching import.

He was back in England for the summers of 1881 and 1882. In the first of those years Gloucestershire had a better season, winning half of their twelve games and losing only two. Midwinter played in every one. He did not bat well—305 runs, with a top score of only 58 against Lancashire—but he took 51 wickets for 897. What is remarkable is that he took wickets in every innings he bowled save one, when he was used but sparingly against Somerset. As usual, he fared well against Yorkshire, with his season's best analysis of seven for 27 in a low-scoring Gloucester victory at Sheffield.

His final season, 1882, was his finest. Gloucestershire had a feeble season: only three wins from thirteen outings and seven defeats. 'Mid', however, topped the averages for the only time, a rare feat with the Graces in the side, and he scored 456 runs for an average of 27. This included his second century for Gloucester (*Wisden* of 1971 is wrong to suggest that he scored but one). This was 107 not out against Somerset, with E. M. Grace scoring 108. *Wisden's* discrepancy may lie in Somerset's status, but *Wisden* of 1883 records the game as part of the County Championship record. He also topped the bowling averages with over 50 wickets—52 for 827, to be exact—including 5 for 59 against Surrey, 6 for 50, almost inevitably at Sheffield, and 5 for 53 and 6 for 66 in separate fixtures with Lancashire.

During these last two English summers he enjoyed good times with the MCC, and, in 1881, he played twice for Players v Gentlemen. 1882 was, as with his county, his best MCC season although, after five main matches, 'he severed his connection with the MCC club rather unexpectedly'. He scored 218 runs (average 36) in these five games, including 137 not out against Derbyshire, whereby he scored more than both Derby innings combined. He took nineteen wickets as well. In a lesser match, he scored 126 not out for A. S. Hayman's XI versus Bristol Medicals, so that *Wisden* records four centuries for him in that season.

His finest was the fourth—187 (his top first-class score) against Leicester for the MCC at Lord's on 1 and 2 June. It amounted to another 'first', for, along with Barnes, he left far behind the previous record wicket-stand. This had been several years earlier—288 by G. F. Grace and I. D. Walker in 1870 for the Southern against the Northern Gentlemen. Now Barnes and Midwinter put Leicester to the sword from ten past four to seven o'clock on the first and from 11.40 to lunch on the second day. In five and a half hours they amassed no less than 454 runs, adding close on 200 to that previous highest, and assembling a record stand which stood for many years. It was noted by the press that 'Mid' played, in comparison with Barnes, 'a more sound innings but his hitting was not so severe'. All things are relative. They maintained a rate of 80 runs an hour overall. As tribute to his phenomenal memory, it was said that during this marathon, he never once lost count of the individual scores of either Barnes or himself! He capped it with a match analysis of seven for 76.

In between-times he toured Australia with Shaw's professional side in 1881-2, and was, according to *Cricket*, 'one of the more useful members of the team'. The promoters did well, coining £1,500 apiece, and the players, too, were well-rewarded. All told, Billy Midwinter took no less than 192 wickets (average 5·6) but only sixteen of these were in first-class matches. He played for England in all four Tests and did moderately well, scoring 95 runs and taking 9

Gentlemen v. Players, 1888

England v. Australia at Lord's, 1896

W. G. Grace bowling, photo by G. W. Beldam

W. G. Grace batting, 1895

Max Beerbohm's cartoon on the occasion of the Testimonial to W. G. Grace following his one hundred hundreds. The artist's caption reads, 'Portrait of Dear old W.G. – to the left is the Grand Stand, to the right, the funeral of one of his patients'

wickets. It was by this means that he became the only man ever to have played for England versus Australia and for Australia versus England.

This subsidised visit to Australia, following his single-handed enterprise of the previous year, must have helped convince 'Mid' that this voyaging from one side of the world to the other had merit. Then, at the end of 1882, *Wisden* recorded in its Gloucester notes that 'one of the mainstays of the XI has returned to Australia for good'.

'Mid' played his last game for Gloucestershire, appropriately enough against the Australians, and travelled back with Murdoch and his men, via the United States—a sure indication that the old troubles were ended. Even so, his proclamation, on landing in Australia, that he was 'heart's core' an Aussie and no kind of Anglo-Australian, was not too well received. One newspaper pondered whether 'another season of vagueness from this very slippery cricketer' was in store. In fact, he never again played for an English team. That very Australian summer he played against Ivo Bligh's English tourists, and was much complimented for his 92 not out against them for Victoria. This led to what *Cricket* called 'the decisive defeat of Mr Bligh's party'. He played once for what was called 'United Australia' against England; that is, once out of a rubber of four.

Some of his 'Test' career was still before him. He travelled to England with Murdoch's team in 1884, still with his old friend Harry Boyle, and with Spofforth still in evidence. He played in all three Tests, including the first ever to be played at Lord's. He took fifteen wickets and had a top score of 46. This was 'Mid's' last visit to the country of his birth. His old 'pupil', Woof, bowled him twice in the matches against his former county, and then he made his last trip across the oceans. He had made something like a dozen such voyages and was, by a very long chalk, the most-travelled cricketer, indeed, sportsman of his day.

These were the bright, central, profitable years for Billy Midwinter, many of them spent under the guidance of and in collaboration with Dr Grace. For Grace's part, these first few years of his medical practice were not, by his own standards, so productive, and there were profound moments of sorrow. Happy in his new-found professional work and with his young family, who found in him a doting father, his cricketing form had been patchy and, save for a strong surge in 1881, Gloucestershire were no longer a major force. Nor was Grace the man to look too kindly on the masterful exploits of the Australians, and in particular their exhilarating 'Ashes' triumph of 1882.

But such anxieties and irritations were overshadowed by two personal tragedies. Less than a month after his historic catching out of Bonnor at the Oval, Fred Grace was dead. Like his father, it began with a chill caused by dampness, an unaired bed at Basingstoke. W.G. and G.F. had been intimates as children and as young cricketing adults. W.G. was closer to G.F. than to his other brothers, and thought of him in terms of deep and genuine affection. The quietest, perhaps the most stylish, certainly the most lovable of the Grace brothers, he was a gifted and elegant cricketer, fluent with bat and as fielder, and he was long mourned. He died on 22 September, and was not yet thirty.

Naturally, his death was equally as wounding to old Mrs Grace. She had had nine children and her life had not always been easy. The pony carriage had given way to a wheel-chair for her visits to cricket matches, and her ceaseless catalogue of her sons' cricketing ventures halted only with her death. That came on 25 July 1884, a week after her seventy-second birthday. In an unprecedented and sensitive gesture A. N. Hornby (with whom W.G. did not enjoy entirely affable relations) stopped the Lancashire and Gloucestershire game at Old Trafford when the news was cabled there. The match was abandoned so that W.G. and Edward could return home to their mother's death-bed.

'The lady in the red cloak' was gone. The little luncheons, with her sons and one or two privileged guests, in her tent at Clifton or Cheltenham, were of the past, but she had outlived her husband long enough to witness the success of their joint labours for their sons and for Gloucestershire. A handsome, if somewhat Spartan, lady in her younger days, she had enjoyed, for that period, a satisfactorily long life. Her later years had been characterised by that stern dignity which one associates with the Victorian grandmother. Indeed, her family can so easily be labelled 'Victorian' that it smacks of a conscious, theatrical effort on their part to obey the literary norms. Professionally and culturally, the Graces occupied and dominated a territory, like some feuding, landowning dynasty. As well as the Graces, there were the Gilberts, the Reeses, the Pococks, and they often intermarried. On one occasion a local match of the tribe was arranged and all twenty-two players were related.

Martha Grace had been the matriarch. Most Sundays the family sub-groups took the lengthy walk to Downend House for lunch. The family Christmas and the midsummer nutting parties could have been borrowed from the pages of *The Pickwick Papers*. They were continued after her mother's death by her daughter Ann, wife of Dr

Skelton. As many as seventy kith and kin might be assembled for such an occasion. The leading members of the clan had developed highly vivid roles: the old father, building a county cricket team around his sons and placing them strategically in medical practices around his, all just prior to his death; the eldest brother, Henry, attempting to sustain family morale; another brother, Edward, grimly maintaining the organisation of the county; Alfred was at Chipping Sodbury, playing some club cricket, but defying the family obsession with his own passion for horses; Gilbert himself, larger than life and stranger than fiction; and the ill-fated younger, Fred, reticent and stylish and much-loved. There were even sub-plots, like Edward's marrying Fred's fiancée after his death: she was the second of his four wives, and with Victorian vigour he sired a sizeable brood of young Graces.

The death of Fred, unexpected and heartrending, and the demise of Martha Grace, unsurprising but no less sad, were hurtful and upsetting for W. G. Grace. Each in their different way—the strictly guiding older hand, the intimate ally and alter ego—left a hollowness in the great cricketer's life, work and sport.

# 8

# W. G. Grace and
# First-class Cricket
# (1885-91)

It was 1885. Gladstone, who, according to Ronald Knox, was one and
the same person as Grace, had been premier again for five years. Grace
himself was thirty-seven years old, and the eldest of his four children,
William Gilbert was, at eleven, beginning to show promise as a runner
and a batsman. And still, year in year out, the practice sessions began
resolutely in early spring, and the cycle of club, county, MCC and
Gentlemen fixtures, with the occasional fillip of a Test match,
wheeled over yet again. Although the power and consistency of his
late twenties was now only rarely achieved, barely a season passed
without vivid, dazzling exhibitions of his greatness. The urge to
master, the unwillingness to submit to the constrictions of tepid
defence, persisted. 'I don't like defensive shots', he said sturdily, 'you
only get threes.'

Like Jacob's brother Esau, he was 'an hairy man'. Like some
Visigoth, hugely bearded and accoutred for battle, he waited expectantly at the wicket, his boot cocked in the arrogant assurance of one
confident that the only poser left was whether the next ball would be
dispatched for three, four or more. Before his innings he took guard,
marking a firm line with a bail, giving notice of permanence. The
muscles of his brawny arms, not unlike those of the village black-
smith, stood out like iron bands. Sleeves rolled to the elbow, the
forearms, like the face, thick with hair, the bat tapping impatient for
mayhem, the enormity of his girth and his very presence, and, atop it
all, pea on a drum, the fast fading red and yellow of his preferred MCC
cap: the image is such that its potency survives and alone among
Victorian sportsmen, and along with precious few from the entire

nineteenth-century pantheon, he is recognisable enough nowadays to be deployed, for instance, cartoon-style in television advertising.

'Tired, jaded humanity', wrote his first biographer in 1887, 'in thousands have left the city and its troubles to come here for a breath of fresh air and the sight of a green field . . . W. G. Grace has had the whole world for a stage, and has it still . . . the centre of attraction on every cricket field, the delight of every lover of the game, and his friends are as numerous as the pebbles on the seashores.'

To some degree, cricket was becoming a more difficult craft. Although wickets were much improved, the guile and accuracy of slow and medium bowling was replacing the array of hazardous but imprecise fast bowlers who had earlier dominated attacks. Batting competition was fiercer. Grace wrote: 'The professional standard of all-round play is higher today than at any time since the game began.' Once asked to name the finest and most reliable batsman of his life-time (himself excluded, after some grave discussion) he cried 'give me Arthur'—namely, the high competence and fluid artistry of Arthur Shrewsbury, the quietly meditative Nottinghamshire batsman.

Yet 1885 was W.G.'s most productive year with the bat since 1876, with over 1,600 runs and an average of 43. Among his half-dozen centuries was a notable and undefeated 221 out of 348 against Middlesex at Clifton. As ever, adversity stirred him to dramatic response: the night previously he had toiled without sleep over a difficult maternity case, prior to conducting his morning surgery. Surrey and, inevitably, Yorkshire watched the runs flow by and around them, and he weighed in with 118 wickets to complete an excellent season. His eighth double, 1,846 runs and 122 wickets, followed in 1886, and in 1887 he scored two centuries in the match against Kent. He was ninth out against Middlesex, with 113 out of 174, and he put Yorkshire to the sword once more with 92 and 193. He scored 1,400 runs (average 63) but took only 63 wickets. He celebrated his fortieth summer, in 1888, with two centuries in one match, also against Yorkshire. 'My champion match', he grandly labelled this one, as, with 148 and 153, he so far outclassed his compatriots that only four other double-figure scores were recorded in both innings. In this fine season he totalled over 2,000 runs and just missed the double, falling seven short of a hundred victims.

Sad to relate, two moderate and one disastrous season followed. In 1889 he had only three centuries, and in 1890 a bad knee—and imag-ine sixteen stones batting on a painful knee—reduced his innings to as few as twenty and his average as low as 19. He scored just one century

## INTERIORS AND EXTERIORS. No. 19.

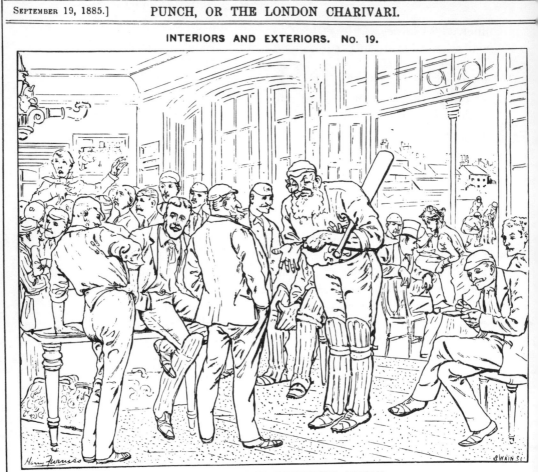

### THE END OF THE CRICKETING SEASON.

A FEW OF THE GENTLEMEN PLAYERS CAUGHT BY OUR ARTIST AT LORD'S.

ATTEND, all ye who love to see our noble Cricket "cracks,"
Here you may get a peep at them, their faces and their backs,
And these are broad, and those are bright, for merry men of muscle
Are they who on our British sward have met in many a tussle.
Foremost stands WILLIAM GILBERT GRACE, he of the raven beard,
By British bowlers dreaded much, by British boys revered.
For twenty years our Champion unchallenged, still he stands
With boyish zeal and nerves of steel, broad shoulders, mighty hands,
Shoulders that "open" smitingly, and hands that never "muff,"
Of whose long scores the cheering "ring" have never *quantum suff.*
How many an English lad, if asked who would he choose to be
Of all our worthies, like a shot would answer—W. G ?
And him to whom Leviathan, low bending, gaily chats,
Pray who is he ?  The great I. D., erst brilliantest of bats.
Sit at the Oval or at Lords, and many an ancient talker,
Will tell you of the wondrous feats lang syne of I. D. WALKER,
Ex-Captain he of Middlesex.  Behold, too, at his side
His smart successor, A. J. WEBBE, aforetime Oxford's pride.
Whilst close behind him, Lancashire's great hero of the bat,
Sits, as the Cockneys know him well a-field "without 'is 'at !"
The dashing A. N. HORNBY.  With his hand upon his hip,
Lord HARRIS stands.  He Kent commands, and seldom a chance let 's
    slip.
Above his shoulder peers the face of W. W. READ,
The boast of Surrey. piler up of scores right few succeed
In topping.  To C. W. WRIGHT, ex-Cantab crack, chats he,
Above them both behold THE STUDD, Cambridge's great C. T.,
Late brilliant bat and bowler grand, to Cricket lost, alas !
Since he to "where Chinesee drive" as preacher pleased to pass.

They do not "drive" as once *he* drove—for sixes.  Cam's great sons
Find yet another member in his neighbour, genial "Buns,"
*The* Slogger C. I. THORNTON, save by BONNOR never beaten,
Who spanked o'er the Pavilion when, a lad, he played for Eton,
And can hit to the next parish when he fairly "lands" a ball.
Lord ! how the groundlings chortle at his hitting clean and tall !
Brilliant O'BRIEN, Oxford's joy, comes next, then Surrey's crack,
The slim and supple DIVER, clean of limb, and straight of back,
Who runs like GEORGE, and throws like Thor.  Next stands his
    Captain smart,
The dashing J. C. SHUTER, who right well has played his part.
Far to the right sits A. G. STEEL, ex-Cantab, master he
Alike of bat and ball, to none save only W. G.
Second, the pride of Lancashire, in style, as skill, A 1.
Close at his back, with curly crop, stands great A. LYTTLETON,
Behind the stumps unbeatable, free bat and slashing field.
Without sits A. P. LUCAS ; he to none afoot need yield
In mingled fire and finish, so correct and clean of play,
All hope upon the tented field to see him many a day.
So *Punch's* pen plays picture-guide, and gives unto the million,
That joy of every Cricketer, a Peep at the Pavilion !

A DANGER FOR DYNAMITERS.—Mr. PARNELL, at a banquet lately
given him, is said to have told his hearers that "he hoped it might
be possible for them to have a platform with only one plank, and
that the plank of national independence."  It is to be hoped that none
of them will, by their acts and deeds, be finally brought to a platform
composed of more planks than one.

for the county versus Kent. It was in that season that E. M. and W. G. Grace reached three figures opening Gloucestershire's batting for the last time together. In a bitter-sweet stand, they assembled 117. Then came 1891. It was W.G.'s most miserable season. In twenty-two innings for the county he could manage only 440 runs at a meagre average of 20. How this impoverishment compared with the abundance of 1887, four years before, when Grace had strung together scores for Gloucestershire in which, during thirteen innings, his lowest score was 20 and he had three centuries and five half-centuries! Apart from persistent knee trouble, he developed a leg strain in mid-season, and finished, with a Homeric nod, nineteenth in the English averages. He managed not a single century.

All this bode ill for Gloucestershire. W.G. had manfully carried the side single-handed so many times, and, when he failed, the county side looked extremely dismal. They slipped to the bottom of the table or thereabouts. In 1887, for example, despite that fine string of Grace innings, they won just one match, and lost nine. The year previously they were almost rock bottom of the county championship for the first time, and, with Grace enjoying but moderate success, the county had little opportunity for rejoicing. The anti-professional attitude of Gloucestershire, to some degree justified by lack of support and funds, did not help. Woof, their loyal left-hand bowler, continued to play and, as the Cheltenham College coach, was pleasantly situated for his role. Fred Roberts, a pacy in-swing bowler, joined him in 1887 as another professional, and Jack Painter, a bowler, had been recruited to the staff in 1882, but, obstreperously, W.G. gave him very little bowling to do. With a paltry attack, reliance was placed on the founder-member and amateur R. F. Miles, who, according to the tactics of the age, bowled off-theory—half-volleys wide of the off stump to a packed and agile offside field.

One cheering aspect was the development of several acres of Ashley Down as Gloucestershire's headquarters at Bristol. Work began in 1887 and on 4 May 1888 a match between the county and the Colts opened the ground. The price paid for the 26-acre site was £6,500 and W.G. was appointed as the first member of the county club to serve on the board of management of 'the Gloucestershire County Ground Co. Ltd.'. The Bristol Rugby Club and the Clifton Association Club were to play their different codes of football on the ground in the winter. W.G. took a fervent interest in the project and grafted away busily on the ground. He never lost his zest for rural activities and he was always ready to roll up his sleeves and prepare to reap and mow and plough and sow. He soon moved house to live close to the ground where some of the grand days of his later career were spent and where the crowds were to fête him. Soon they were to build the County Ground Hotel nearby simply because on a handful of days each summer W. G. Grace would stalk to the middle and bat. His liveliness never deserted him. In 1887 the festival match at Scarborough between the MCC and Yorkshire ended early, and boisterous games of soccer and rugby were quickly arranged. W.G. was in the van. At nearly forty, he laid on two goals in the first and scored a scorching try in the second.

The Australians maintained their visits to England, just as, conversely, English teams sailed southwards practically every winter. In the winters of 1884/5 and 1886/7 strong professional sides visited Australia, with Shrewsbury, W. Barnes, Lohmann and Peel proving too strong for their opponents, particularly on the second tour. The winter after, 1887/8, in what seems to be a frenzy of over-enthusiasm, two sets of tourists—Lord Hawke's team at the invitation of Melbourne Cricket Club and Arthur Shrewsbury on another of his business trips—arrived. The financial consequences were disastrous, but the cricket was successful, from the English viewpoint, with the elegant A. E. Stoddart charming the Australian crowds for the first time.

Perhaps the leading characteristic of so-called international cricket at this time was the deterioration of Australian cricket physically and morally. Torn by internecine squabbles, almost all of them motivated by monetary considerations, their cricket became frail and ineffective. From the beginning of 1886 to 1890 the Australians lost ten out of their next eleven fixtures with England. H. J. H. Scott's team of 1886 lost the Test at Old Trafford all but entirely due to Barlow's batting and bowling. Then they were annihilated, twice, by an innings. At the Oval W.G. and the dour stonewaller, Scotton, put on 170 for the first wicket. W.G. went on to score the highest by an Englishman in Tests on home soil until 1921. W.G. considered this innings carefully. He described it as 'not altogether faultless but ... without undue cynicism, a pretty good performance'. That season he also scored centuries for the Gentlemen and for Gloucester against the Australians.

In 1888 Percy McDonnell and the sixth Australians embarked on another tour, and Grace had the honour for the first time of captaining his country. Turner and Ferris took 534 wickets in another damp summer, and the Australians won their one victory at Lord's, only to lose the other two Tests by an innings: Murdoch brought over a side two years later in 1890, but, again, it was inexperienced and raw.

There was more bad weather and not a ball was bowled in the Old Trafford Test. England won the other two easily enough. It was a grim period for Australia, but W.G., who played in every one of the home Tests, was hugely delighted by the whole business. He scored a hundred against them for the Gentlemen in 1888.

It was during the 1886/7 tour of Australia that W. G. Grace's old partner, Billy Midwinter, had that one last twist to his 'Test' career. He played against Shrewsbury's side in both internationals, completing his unchallenged and unique record. In total, he played four times for England and eight times for Australia, all but three of these games being played in Australia. He had, of course, benefited socially as well as financially from his days in England. As *Cricket* said, he 'acquired no small degree of polish'; rough and ready he may have been, 'but his contact with people more refined had a salutary effect'. Like more famous professionals, such as Shaw and Shrewsbury, Midwinter examined the socio-economic frame of cricket very carefully. He used it, solid Victorian that he was, to boost his own prospects. Despite the class formation of English cricket, it offered, as did all facets of Victorian life, occasional opportunities for upward mobility. His acceptance as an MCC professional is further testimony to this point— for such status a certain social poise was required.

It may have been the key to improved social conditions for the Shrewsburys and the Midwinters, and certainly Grace himself was no economic loser through cricket, but for W.G. as for many others, the motivation was also that of cricket as a character-builder. In an article in the *Boy's Own Paper*, under the title of 'Cricket and How to Excel in it', he wrote sternly: 'Remember that the game is not the mere triviality it is sometimes taken to be, but is worth thinking about, worth doing well, and that, as in everything else, intelligent practice and perseverance are the secret of success.' This practice was to be for four hours for a group of sixteen with eleven in the field, two batting, two bowling, two umpiring and one scoring on a conveyor-belt roster. Everyone had fifteen minutes batting, however many times 'out', bowling and so forth, with a simple enough procedure for computing the scores. He stoutly recommended 'long stopping' as 'a capital school for general fielding', and he roundly condemned the balls 'many of our so-called bowlers deliberately throw'; an opinion not likely to endear him to the professional bowlers. As for batting, 'Shift your left foot in hitting as much as you like, but be cautious of moving your right ... your defence principally depends on your right foot remaining stationary.' W.G. always laid great store on the solid pivot of his back foot, depending solely on the swift and incisive movement of his front leg. He also liked, he wrote, grounds which measured 200 yards across either way, somewhat larger than the 70-yard boundaries of the present day. 'The larger the ground', he opined, 'the fewer the boundary hits, and the better the game.' He also had a piece of canny advice for the readers of the *Boy's Own Paper*: 'Never lend your favourite bat', he told them, 'you will break it quite soon enough yourself.'

Occasionally his joint careers coincided. In 1887 at Manchester the Oxford blue A. C. M. Croome, fielding on the boundary, pierced his throat on the sharp railing. W. G. Grace saved his life by holding together the gaping wound for some thirty minutes before more sophisticated assistance could be brought. In 1890 L. J. M. Fox dislocated his shoulder while fielding for Kent: E. M. Grace sat on his head while W.G., with one foot against his body, yanked his arm until the shoulder bone was replaced. Curiously, poor Fox had a repetition of this at Bristol. W.G. was not playing on that occasion, so E.M. recruited two Kentish stalwarts as aides. W.G. also treated his own players, on one occasion setting Fred Roberts's badly dislocated thumb out on the field.

As for his own surgery, he made it quite clear to Gloucestershire that it could not be deserted absolutely while he played cricket for them. Such was his contribution to the shire's cause that the authorities had to make amends, such as paying for a locum as his assistant. Although Gloucestershire were hard pressed for money, and argued incessantly over players' expenses, it would have been a false economy not to oblige Grace, for he was their economic, as he was their sporting, guarantee. Soon after he became a doctor the county minutes record how £20 was set aside for this purpose and, in a year or so, £36. These are not large sums, even when assessed by the money values of the time, but they indicate a payment in kind to the 'Big Doctor' and an illustration of how the purity of amateurism was sullied. There was no sense in which, however, Grace could be thought of socially as a professional. His whole approach was so different to, for instance, that of James Southerton, of whom *Wisden*, referring to his benefit match in 1880, said 'He is always civil to those who occupy a superior social position to himself, without in the least degree being servile.'

As well as being captain of Gloucestershire, W.G. was now captain of England. Professionals might organise touring parties abroad, but, at home, this was, of course, out of the question. Having played under

Lord Harris in 1879, 1880 and 1884, and under his long-standing and not too friendly rival A. N. Hornby in 1882, and under A. G. Steel, like Hornby, a gifted Lancashire amateur, in 1886, W.G. in his fortieth year was elevated to the captaincy. Apart from two matches when Steel and Stoddart respectively deputised, he captained England in home Tests from 1888 to 1896, twelve matches in all. Why was he rejected as captain until so late in his career? After all, he had captained sides since his early twenties, and had proved a most successful county skipper ever since Gloucester had achieved first-class status. There was no argument about his tactical know-how, which was highly shrewd and sophisticated; some would have said a little too much so. His inspirational performance and presence as a leader were by-words. It may have been recalled that he was not too affectionately disposed toward the old enemy and was, to say the least, lacking in diplomatic subtleties. It may also have been pointed out that he was not always the darling of the top-class professionals and was not perhaps the man to command their political respect, much as they grudgingly appreciated his sporting prowess.

But the chief reason, and one difficult to separate from the other rationalisations, may well have been the class difficulty. Lord Harris, the fourth earl, of Oxford University and Kent and the two Lancastrian amateurs, Hornby, the gifted Harrovian, and Steel of Marlborough and Cambridge University were reputable English captains. Grace, the country doctor, straying a little too closely near the professional line, was not of this ilk, and, once more, the lack of public school, university and wealthy family must have rankled. Not until he was a mature and well-nigh middle-aged statesman-cricketer was he permitted that privilege.

The counties, by now, had established their identity completely, and the MCC had, in its turn, guaranteed its own authority. Often the amateurism was like the driven snow: the Surrey amateur, Edward Dawson, claimed that that county's amateurs received not a penny, not even for hotel and railway expenses. And, as the stream of talented amateurs continued, it was quite possible for teams like Middlesex and Kent and, if now to a lesser extent, Gloucestershire, to prosper without overmuch recourse to paid players.

The county championship still showed signs of being a cavalier and rather dilettante tournament, as if to structure it too formally would reek of an overweening seriousness about results. From 1873, when some primitive regulations of eligibility, including only playing for one county in a full season, were established, there was some form of a league, but it was tentative and uncertain. There were varying numbers of games and varying types of assessment, from 'least defeats' to 'most victories'. During the 1880s county matches doubled to fifty in a season, but it was not until the 1890s that the custom of each county playing the others 'home' and 'out' was introduced. By the end of the century about 150 county matches were being played. But there was no proper distinction between first- and second-class counties until 1886 and it was only in 1890 that a points system was agreed for the championship.

In 1887 a self-constituted County Cricket Council was formulated to deal with knotty queries about qualification and classification, the deadly duo as far as county cricket was concerned. In 1890 (once more following football's lead: the Football League began operations in 1888) this council suggested three divisions or classes, with, as was the Football League fashion, a sudden-death home and away play-off of bottom of the upper and top of the lower tier. This was much opposed by the second-string counties and the council disbanded itself in 1890. By 1894 the counties had surrendered full rights to the MCC.

For W. G. Grace, an unmitigated opponent of county autonomy and, for a man of his bluff independence of spirit, practically a sycophantic adherent to the MCC cause, the final collapse of cricket's 'Parliament' was a moment of rejoicing. He spoke and wrote volubly, for him, of the rare qualities of MCC as a fount of cricketing sovereignty. His adherence to that cause seems strange. One might have expected some support for the more provincial and broadly based cause from that staunchest of west countrymen. Conversely, Grace's suspicions of what he regarded as the over-professionalisation of some teams and his distinctly uneasy relations with some of his amateur colleagues in other counties may help to explain this. Certainly the Grace family thought county cricket had progressed far enough. W.G. had also been well-treated by the MCC. As someone who sailed close to the wind of both sporting controversy and financial probity, the club had been remarkably lenient with him. His rows with visiting Australians and others had not unduly concerned the club, while they had—as on the occasion of his testimonial—encouraged rather than the reverse his making money from the sport.

By the end of the Victorian era, and with Grace its fervent ally, the MCC was all-powerful. Ostensibly a private club, it had fastened its grip on the first-class game and was regarded as its oracle, and as far as the counties themselves were concerned, a non-partisan arbitrator was as sane a solution as could be devised. In these conditions amateur talent flowered and by the end of the century magical names were appearing: the stylish Lionel Palairet, the supremely confident F. S. Jackson, the majestic Archie MacLaren, the shrewdly analytical Charles Fry, the dynamic Gilbert Jessop, the regally fluent Reggie Spooner; above all, perhaps, in his grip on popular imagination, the sinuously graceful Ranjitsinhji. All of these, and there were many more, were products of public school or university, and most of them of both.

The family background which enabled them to flourish in boarding school and varsity normally meant that, unlike Grace, they commanded the wealth which permitted them to play cricket for free and for pleasure. Although one or two, Fry and Spooner are instances, could not find the time to tour abroad, the general disposition of family business and estates accorded them rich leisure time for their cricket. It is often argued that the more carefree approach of the amateur brought untold colour and vitality to the game, and certainly Jessop's normal scoring rate of eighty an hour would be much too tempestuous for today's cricketers. What is certain is that, in the forty years before World War I as spectator sports grew in importance, this tide of gifted amateurs following in the wake of Grace, were very much part of that entertainment. When England played Australia in 1902, Johnny Tyldesley (significantly, one of the most gallant and breathtaking of professional batsmen) was the only paid specialist batsman, the other five being MacLaren, Jessop, Jackson, Ranji and Fry. In 1900 only two professionals appeared in the first twenty in the first-class batting averages.

The professional bowlers who journeyed to Oxford or Cambridge at the commencement of the season to provide high-grade practice, and those other professionals, such as H. H. Stephenson at Uppingham or W. A. Woof at Cheltenham, who became coaches, were the nurserymen for these triumphant batsmen. The old 'pro', treated with great respect and affection at the public school nets, is a stereotype of the age. These were the men who schooled the MacLarens and the Spooners into becoming such formidable performers in the classic tradition. From an early age they were taught to play impeccably, and, whilst the grandest among them added their own individualist stamp, this was the key. Moreover, these were not wayward nor instinctive geniuses. It was in keeping with the sterling application one associates with Victorianism, that men like Ranji and Fry worked and practised with indefatigable patience.

And it is fair to say that, had Grace been of a contemplative disposition he might have surveyed the first-class cricketing scene as the 1890s opened, and meditated that, head and shoulders above everyone else, he was its progenitor.

That, certainly, is the view of C. L. R. James in his *Beyond a Boundary*, one of cricket's finest and wisest pieces of literature. In as carefully a judged assessment as has been attempted, James wrote of Grace, 'He did what no one else had ever done, developed to a degree unprecedented, and till then undreamt of, potentialities inherent in the game....It was by modern scientific method that this pre-Victorian lifted cricket from a more or less casual pastime into the national institution which it rapidly became. Like all truly great men, he bestrides two ages.'

# 9
# W. G. Grace: Australia Revisited (1891/2)

Lord Sheffield, President of Sussex and a tireless devotee of cricket, managed to persuade W.G. to undertake a second and final tour of Australia over the winter of 1891/2. His wife, as on the first trip, his daughter and his youngest son accompanied him. But leaving some of his family and his patients for so long was something of a wrench: one had to be away many months and W.G. was no sailor. The desire, however, to attack the enemy on their own battleground, while he was still England's official skipper, must have been strong. He must have realised too that it would probably be his last opportunity so to do, and have reasoned that some sort of pick-me-up was in order after the moderate success of recent seasons. The £3,000, generous expenses and a locum for the practice must have helped to persuade the country doctor, anxious as he was to provide his children with the kind of social and educational background which his amateur colleagues had enjoyed.

So off he sailed in the autumn of 1891. It was a reasonably strong side, although it lacked the power of Gunn and Shrewsbury. Stoddart was available and in good form, and Bobby Abel, the Surrey batsman, was to have a successful tour. Attewell of Notts, Briggs of Lancashire and Lohmann of Surrey, although past his prime, were the leading bowlers.

One possible pleasure was to be denied him: that of meeting up with or playing against his erstwhile team-mate, Billy Midwinter. He was a winter too late. The year after 'Mid' re-settled in Australia he had married. His bride was Elizabeth Frances McLaughlan, and they married in Melbourne in the June of 1883. W. E. Midwinter was then aged thirty-two. He still played cricket, but his professional days, at least in any overt sense, were ending. It was still said that 'there were few more vigorous hitters', that he had 'unusual reach', that his medium (no longer fast-medium) bowling demonstrated 'considerable work from the off', and that he was 'a sure catch and threw well'. Having made money and gained self-assurance over the last six years, the newly married 'Mid' was ready to venture into business. Rather vaguely, his early endeavours are variously described as 'mining transactions' and 'stockbroking'. It was certainly no sedentary occupation, and he probably followed his father's footsteps into the minefields. Once, whilst camping on the plains and 'after a long and exhausting walk', he pitched tent and slept through a storm during which the water rose four inches. He 'never suffered the slightest effect from it', given a 'constitution marvellously strong'.

However, none of this was successful—either W. E. Midwinter overreached himself or lacked good fortune. His cricket continued. He played for East Melbourne, when they won the M'Clean Cup, for Carlton CC, his old club, and finally for South Melbourne CC. He was considered competent enough to be invited to tour England with P. S. McDonnell's team in 1888, but his eyes were, he felt, fading and his business matters, or so he pleaded, were pressing. By now he had turned to what was the prototypical and often fatal vocation of the ex-cricketer, that of publican. He had as many pubs as cricket clubs, first as 'boniface' of the Clyde Hotel, Carlton, then on to the South Melbourne Hotel, and finally to the Victoria Hotel, in Melbourne's Bourke Street, a large and prosperous hostelry. About this time his eyes really did become troublesome, and he dropped out of cricket completely. Nonetheless, his shrewd grasp and experience of the game, and his highly diverting mode of discussing it, meant that he was in some demand in cricket circles as adviser and exemplar. But Harry Boyle had already noted, in 1888, 'certain peculiarities in his manner'.

It would appear that, for the few years he was a landlord, he made money 'and looked after it pretty carefully'. Like his mentor, W. G. Grace, Billy Midwinter had a sharp eye for money. At a time when a police constable earned about £100 a year, he had earned £300 to £400 in an English season. He probably earned not much less in a normal Australian season and then there were collections and 'his usual share of the gate money' on top of his £15 or £16 a week. At Scarborough the spectators had once offered 'improvised proof' of their appreciation. He showed 'great relish of his trouble in counting it'. It took him two hours to count that £30 collection into a carpet bag, the largest coin being a sixpence. In itself that indicates not only the breadth of appreciation but the size of the crowd. Such a prosperous professional may well have earned £750 to £1,000 a year in those central years of his career and although it fails to compare with the wealth accumulated by Grace, it still remains, in Victorian working-class terms, a substantial achievement.

But within twelve months, three dreadful domestic tragedies struck which unhinged a mind already—if Boyle is to be believed—a trifle disturbed. Midwinter's baby daughter, Elsie, died of pneumonia at the end of 1888; his wife died of apoplexy the following summer, and, in the November of 1889, just a year after Elsie's untimely death, his three-year-old son, Albert Ernest, also died. The following June, while staying with relations, he became violent, and after a short spell in Bendigo hospital, had to be committed to the Kew Asylum in Melbourne. He was paralysed from the waist down and often comatose.

Despite his desperate condition, W. E. Midwinter was able to rally sufficiently to do what all cricketers enjoy and to chew the cricketing fat for an hour or so with old colleagues, like Harry Boyle, when they visited him. But within a fortnight he was dead. He died on 3 December 1890, and two days later his funeral was attended by a considerable following of his fellow sportsmen, among them the Gloucester amateur W. O. Tonge, who had played alongside 'Mid' in the county side. He was buried in Melbourne General Cemetery, beside his wife and his two tiny children, where they lay—his wife being of that religion—in the Roman Catholic sector of that burial ground. He was just a few months past his thirty-ninth birthday. He had established the last of his 'firsts', and that a macabre one. He was the first international or 'Test' cricketer to die.

*Haygarth's Scores and Biographies* mourned him: 'May the death of no other cricketer who has taken part in great matches be like his' and *Cricket* woefully commented that 'pale death has lately removed a cricketer whose form was almost if not quite as well known on English as on Australian grounds'.

It was a depressingly sad end to an interesting if low-key sporting life. Because Grace was so gargantuan a character, he is not so much the prototype as the creator of Victorian cricket. Midwinter is more typical, and because of his breadth of experience and the sometimes strong link with Grace, he managed to embrace most of the features of Victorian cricket. He was essentially Victorian: aspiring, self-assured, a vigorous professional, a perky raconteur, something of a dissimulator and never less than watchful where money was concerned. In that vigorous if often hypocritical society, he had made his way admirably and pragmatically.

By now Australia's population was some 3 millions, a quarter residing in the two chief cities, and, from 1875 to 1880, in a repeat of England's railway mania, the rail mileage sprang from 1,000 to 4,000 and kept rising. Australia was becoming subject to American as well as English influences, adopting the telegraph and the telephone very soon after England, and, in general, was a highly urbanised and industrialised society.

Materially Australia was Britain with a bonus. The bonus amounted normally to a fair prosperity with, it was claimed, most workmen eating three meals of meat a day. Material contentment embraced leisure time. The eight-hour day and the half-day Saturday were now the rule in Australia, allowing time to practise or watch cricket. With two-thirds of the population living in towns, the typical Australian life-style lay in the suburbs rather than the outback. The sewing machine and the lawnmower made faster progress in Australia than in Britain. Put another way, Australia practically out-Britained Britain as an urbanised, industrialised state. A common view of cricket is that it evolved as a pastoral sport in England and then was transmitted to a huge agrarian colony. In fact, it came of age as an urban game in this country and was taken up in the new and growing conurbations of that second new world.

And sport mattered fearfully. Apart from cricket, there was horse-racing: crowds of 80,000 would assemble for the Melbourne Cup, equalling a third of that city's population. Sport was the one colonial career open to all the talents. 'Not to be interested in cricket,' opined one commentator, 'amounts almost to a social crime'. Crowds stood almost all night outside newspaper offices awaiting the scores as they came over the cables. The concept of the 'Beach Democracy' and the muscular, courageous athlete was promoted. Australians regarded as heroic not only excellence at games but more particularly excellence at English games. Apart from the scarcely popular Victorian Rules Football, Australia never invented a sport of its own. It made do with England's, adopting cricket, then with immense speed within months of their appearance as sports, cycling and swimming. Australia won the Davis Cup for tennis in 1908. The 'Englishness' of Victorian Australia must be stressed again. Nowadays the Australian temperament and approach are seen as very different from Britain's, but in the period when Test Match cricket developed it was this flattering mimicry which was dominant.

Not unnaturally, Australia was the most enthusiastic focus for the New Imperialism in the thirty or so years before World War I. Australia had its Imperial Federation League; it was an Australian, W. H. Fitchett, who wrote the best-seller, *Deeds that Won the Empire*, and 400,000 Australian troops went to France in World War I, of whom 80,000 were slain and 200,000 wounded. The imperial cult was heavily religious as well as jingoistic: as Alfred Austin, the poet laureate, put it: 'who dies for England, sleeps with God'.

Cricket was the sport of the imperialists. It had been and continued to be used as a colonising technique. It was proof positive of the empire builder's blue blood. It was an exhibition of Englishness, a badge to flaunt and a belief to celebrate. In tandem, the method is best illustrated by India, with the British playing cricket to testify to their heritage and the Indians playing it to demonstrate how British they had become. Australia was, however, still the major arena for the Empire at play, and, naturally, it was the tours to and from England around which this developed. The tremendous extension of the railway system made the 1891/2 tour much easier on the players' stamina than the one of eighteen years previously, and what has been called 'his bulk and his buoyancy' made Grace a popular figure. Baths were still not plentiful over that sweltering terrain, but Grace, for a medical man, was not overfond of soapy water. On one occasion he snapped, 'We Graces ain't no bloody water spaniels.'

The English found the Australians, under the leadership of their wicket-keeper, J. McC. Blackham, emerging from long years of doldrums. Spofforth and J. J. Ferris now lived in England, but Ferris's old bowling partner C. T. B. Turner, 'The Terror', was still in evidence. The highly competent all-rounder (he once scored 271 and took sixteen for 166 for South Australia) George Giffen was available, the most talented player of those involved in the rows over the last decade. It was the batting which showed unprecedented signs of doggedness and stability. Alex Bannerman was the doughtiest and most resourceful. In every one of the three Tests he batted with patience and resolve, once taking seven and a half hours over 91. Lyons hit with abandon in every game to complement Bannerman's sturdy defence, and the Australians won the first two Tests. The English retaliated with a spanking victory in the third game, but the Australians were well pleased. The adrenalin had begun to flow once more.

The doctor was in fine form. He reached his only first-class century outside the British Isles when he scored 159 against Victoria at

Melbourne. But Grace and the Australians were never quite to enjoy harmonious relations. There were constant 'wrangles', to use W.G.'s own word. There were wrangles about who should umpire; there were wrangles over disputed catches; there was the case of Grace leading his men off one field because of the nastiness of the wicket. Indeed it is difficult to find a tour of Australia by England, or vice versa, in this era which was not beset by 'wrangles'. Alfred Shaw, who acted as manager on the trip and who by now was an experienced organiser, reported that the sponsor, Lord Sheffield, spent £16,000 on the tour, at a net loss of £2,000. Money, matches, prestige and good fellowship were all lost; the chief gain was a restoration of Australia's flagging fortunes, for, as ever, lack of success had begotten lack of interest over the preceding years.

Like a Julius Caesar or a Napoleon, W.G. was as eager for foreign conquests as he was for domestic pre-eminence. He played every match, as he was contracted to do, and, did any finish early, exhibition matches, with Grace the centrepiece, were speedily arranged. This insistence on his daily performance was unlike previous tours where the amateurs had enjoyed leisure pursuits, leaving the professionals to soldier on match after match. On this occasion Grace was treated strictly as the profitable asset, so much so that almost a fifth of the gross cost of the tour was his huge fee.

Australia still remained the most important focus for cricket outside England. Cricket was, of course, played in other countries under English dominion, but little of it was in the same class. It advanced fitfully in New Zealand, which was, in population, no more than another Australasian colony, and, despite the army's presence in South Africa, development was not too brisk there: it was 1888/9 before an English side visited and found South African standards abysmal. Military and official personnel helped introduce the sport into both India and the West Indies, and the indigenous populations took readily to cricket, but the fruits of this were to be a long time ripening. Having produced its one top-class player, John Barton King, the pace-bowler, North America had languished as far as cricket was concerned, and no European country played cricket at any reasonable first-class standard. The upshot was that, apart from four tours to South Africa during which usually under-strength English teams annihilated the South Africans on the eight occasions they clashed, no other international cricket was played in the nineteenth century apart from England and Australia. In fact it was 1928 before England added a third opponent, the West Indies, to its exclusive fixture list.

It is important to an assessment of Grace and his contemporaries to realise that the international is scarcely a hundred years old, and, initially, lacked much of today's ideological passion and national frenzy. Even the paradoxically termed 'home' internationals in soccer and rugby date only from the 1870s. The professional cricketer—Billy Midwinter is a perfect example—was, in the best sense, a mercenary, motivated to sell his expertise at the best price. That does not mean he was or is cynical or disloyal but that he had, like other kinds of professionals, to balance his priorities carefully. A shrewder reading of the activities of such players might have helped the 1970s cricket establishment to comprehend and cope with the Packer crisis more sensitively.

The very composition of national sides was open to question. The early touring sides, for instance, may have been the select of England, but, if and when they were, it depended on the bargaining and diplomatic skill of the promoter. It was late in the century before the selection of national teams was subjected to the scrutiny of a national controlling body. In fact the very term 'Test match' was originally used as early as the 1860s each time an English party played a colony, such as New South Wales or Victoria, and it was only with Arthur Shrewsbury's tour of 1884 that the label affixed itself to England-Australia games. As for that first historic encounter in 1877, W. G. Grace—and it would be difficult to find a safer judge than he—defined it accurately as when 'an Australian eleven for the first time beat an eleven of England'. The emphasis is on the number, the fact that they won even-handedly as opposed to using fifteen players, and on the indefinite articles—*an* Australian eleven and *an* eleven of England.

Thereafter the tours, on both sides, were money-making ventures, rarely able to attract the best available players. Grace visited Australia only twice; Ranji and Jessop went but once; Fry and Spooner never made the trip at all. What is equally critical is whether games can be properly termed internationals when the methods of selection were so peculiar. The tours to Australia were more or less privately arranged, and often completely professional in personnel, while, for 'Tests' in this country, it was the county committee at the relevant venue who invited players to form a side. Archie MacLaren is said to have stood in one dressing room surrounded by abashed players as he glanced at his team-sheet, struck his brow in anguish and sighed 'oh, no, no' as he read some of the names. Ranji himself was excluded at Lord's in 1896, some thought because of racial prejudice, although he played in all the other Tests, and his nephew Duleepsinhji also suffered this embarrassment a generation later. It was the summer of 1899, when, with five home 'Tests' for the first time, the oddity of the situation had to be faced. A MCC Board of Control was formed to pick sides in England. Then, in 1903, under Pelham Warner's captaincy, the first MCC side visited Australia.

Australia, like England, also developed its own official national body. In 1891/2 the Australasian Cricket Council had been formed in an atmosphere of warring factions based on strongly autonomous state and city clubs. This collapsed in 1900, to be succeeded in 1905 by the Australian Board of Control for Cricket. This agency firmly took control of matters such as the selection for and management of tours. It countered the abrasive player power which had sometimes tarnished the image of Australian cricket and was prepared in the season 1911/12 to take strong measures with several recalcitrant players. In a word, it was really 1905 before Australia followed England's suit and established a self-perpetuating oligarchy which fought for acceptance as the sovereign body.

This is not an argument in favour of the MCC and the Australian Board having and enjoying these wide powers. Sometimes their approach has seemed less objective and more idiosyncratic than the private enterprise of an Alfred Shaw or the joint whims of, for instance, the Nottinghamshire committee for the Trent Bridge Test. When, in 1909, twenty-five players were recruited over the home series, lost by England two to one, with two draws, there were many such complaints. What is being argued is that, until a *bona fide* national organisation existed, it is misleading to talk of international cricket. As it is, as many as seventy-one games are recognised by most authorities as official 'Tests' before some form of national agency had overall supervision in *both* countries.

From a purist viewpoint, then, one might say that W.G. and Spofforth (to say nothing of Billy Midwinter) never played in an inter-national match. One even wonders whether the somewhat arbitrary consideration of what does in fact constitute a Test match in the official litany was concerned more with including the exploits of these pioneers, despite the dread convention of professional captains, than with legitimacy. Maybe that appreciation of the spirit rather than the letter of the law is right; however, there must have been many cricket-lovers who, when asked to celebrate the centenary test in January of 1977, believed they were commemorating a match between two official national teams.

What that centenary celebrated was more the spread of an imperialist cult, for significant cricket has not been played outside areas of English colonisation. It is sometimes suggested that cricket is essentially 'English' and that its peculiar tempo, its complicated regimen and its strange social manners make it somehow exclusively Anglo-Saxon. Alternatively, one might argue that north European territories, such as Germany or Holland, are more similar to England than England is, say, to the Indian sub-continent or the West Indies, and cricket is much more the province of the West Indians than of the Scots or Irish.

It seems likelier that cricket is essentially Victorian, or Victorian-English, rather than purely English. The cricket played around Philadelphia and parts of Canada in the nineteenth century testifies to this. It was when the economic pace of North American life quickened and when its social mores radically changed, not least because of the influx of continental Europeans, that cricket drooped in the United States and in Canada. This may partly be concerned with the heavy-handed class pattern of Victorian cricket. Australia, despite its American influences, was much more determined to reproduce the English manner than the Americans and Canadians. In India, South Africa and in the West Indies, something of the same social hegemony was accepted, and this, of course, had an ethnic as well as a social character. What was important was that colonisation and cricket reached their highest watermarks at the same time.

Timing was of the essence. Precisely as English Imperialism made its bid to imprint its stamp on its overseas possessions, cricket was available to form part of the mould. Contrariwise, it was as precisely when that Imperialism was decaying, particularly in the aftermath of World War I, that football emerged dramatically as the grand global game, but too late for the colonies and dominions to be much attracted. It was in 1930 that the first football World Cup competition was held.

In 1909 the Imperial Cricket Conference was formed, purportedly to run world cricket, significant because it was five years later than football's equivalent, and, unlike FIFA, it was by no means on a worldwide basis. Indeed, only the South African Cricket Association for *white* cricketers, the Australian Board of Control and the MCC were members, and the lobbying had been initiated by South Africa where, as Rowland Bowen points out in his *Cricket: A History of its Growth and Development throughout the World*, the wasteful damage of sporting apartheid stretched back to the 1890s. It was labelled Imperial, and imperial it remained. It was 1925 before New

Zealand, West Indies and India were admitted to the conference. Forty or so years later, in 1965, 'Imperial' became 'International'.

Thus the three oligarchic committees of England, Australia and South Africa supervised world cricket as the new century dawned, virtually ensuring that the old-style 'colonial' approach would remain dominant. It was a dominance, which, in turn, helped guarantee that cricket would never, like football, tear free from this imperialistic shackle and become a global sport.

The historical features of imperialist cricket are, therefore, deep-rooted and important. W. G. Grace may not have had the happiest of relationships with the Australians and may at times have bristled with outrage at what he regarded as their improprieties. But as Grace was early to accept when the war came, this was dramatised play, and the likes of Germany were the genuine enemy. Grace was regarded by the Australians with a mixture of awed respect and veiled antagonism. It was not entirely unlike the way the missionaries and empire-builders were regarded by their clientele. W.G., as a Test cricketer, must have been seen in an imperialist rather than an international mould. In his own second-phase field, Grace might better be classified with David Livingstone and Cecil Rhodes.

# 10
# W. G. Grace to his Indian Summer (1892-5)

Grace returned to England from his second Australian tour, and, as is often the way with that kind of experience, he was part refreshed and part jaded. The hardship of sea and land travel, although not so burdensome as on his first visit, and the sheer concentration of playing cricket, travel apart, three consecutive seasons as the man under the public microscope was, of course, exhausting. On the other hand he had enjoyed all manner of personal success and, as was his wont, he had indulged his hearty appetite for innocent glory and pleasure with keen satisfaction.

Once more he settled down to that extraordinary double life of being a humdrum, run-of-the-mill general practitioner in the restricted locale he knew so well, and, for a third of his time being the world's most celebrated sportsman. He was a mellow and affectionate family man, and, like so many huge, extrovert, loud, triumphant men, he was gentle and kindly and patient with children. Throughout his life this knack of relating sympathetically to youngsters, especially toddlers, was never marred by the shortness and infelicity which characterised some of his relationships with adults.

His own family were fast growing. During the summer of his return Bertie was eighteen, Edgar was sixteen, Bessie was fourteen and Charles was ten. They commanded much of the attention that remained when sporting and professional matters had been considered. The one exception was the 'sacred night or two' of whist, which he played with fellow doctors. Non-intellectual to the point of caricature (what A. A. Thomson called his 'amiable neglect of literature and politics'), Grace devoured all he could find printed on the arcane mysteries of whist.

Bertie and Edgar were day-boys at Clifton. Their father had not plunged them into the deep end of the public school, despite his respect for its products. This was a half-way step, as if he was anxious, like his own father, to keep a domesticated eye on their development. So they walked to and from school each day and, what is more, they walked home and back for lunch—altogether fourteen miles a day. Both boys were diligent at their books. Like their father, they were hard-working but not intellectually bright. Like their father, they were keen on running as well as cricket. They both opted to be sprinters, and Bessie, too, was a quick runner and evidently a cheery and refreshing young lady as well.

According to A. G. Powell, 'the younger ''W.G.'' looked more of the student than the athlete'. He was a tall youth, bespectacled, cool in disposition, diffident in manner. He was very unlike the prototypical Grace, talkative, boisterous and assured; and, in spite of the most intensive instruction and coaching from childhood, he never overcame a rigidity and awkwardness of style. A fractured arm early in his career did nothing to help, although, like his father and uncles, the garden practice pitch was the focus for his boyhood leisure.

In his last year at Clifton he was captain of school, of cricket and of football. He batted with good sense for an average of 29 and he took 51 wickets for the school XI. That year—1893—he made his first appearance for the county on the college ground, but managed only a duck and a meagre 11 runs in his two knocks against Middlesex. He played two or three other games that season with similar consequences. He then fulfilled another facet of his father's ambition for him by going to Pembroke College, Cambridge. W.G. was thrilled to hear of his son's success in the Freshmen's trial match, but, unluckily, form of any kind deserted him, and he failed to get his Blue. But there was one compensating feature in the summer of 1894. W.G. had scored 139 for the MCC against Cambridge at Fenners, as if chastising the University for ill-treating his offspring. A month later he scored a further 196, his highest-ever score at Lord's, for the MCC against the Cantab bowling, and, on this second occasion, there was a long stand between father and son, with the boy scoring a sound fifty. It must have given W.G. great joy to bat at length with his eldest son, at Lord's and against the University, especially as Bertie had had two ducks in these two MCC games. They played on the same side many times, but they never managed again any joint success. One August Bank Holiday in front of a large crowd against Sussex at Ashley Down, for instance, they opened the batting: W.G. Junior 1, W.G. Senior 301.

However, 1895 was the boy's best year, just as it proved to be so special for his father. It was the cherry on the iced cake of that splendid summer for W. G. Grace when young Bertie opened the Cambridge innings with Frank Mitchell, the talented Yorkshire amateur. His father was puffed with glee and pride, quite as genuinely delighted with his son's moderate success as with his own triumphs of that summer. He had a private box for the occasion and celebratory drinks.

He was not to prosper, however. He obtained another Blue next year, in 1896, but was dismissed for nought in each innings. He played for Gloucestershire occasionally over another two or three years, but, neither as batsman nor bowler, did he really reach county standard. His best first-class score was 62 against Nottinghamshire. It was a grave disappointment to the older Grace.

W.G.'s two other sons, Edgar and Charles, who played for Clifton College, were not destined to be first-class cricketers, and although the other Edgar, one of E.M.'s several children, played occasionally for MCC, he never made the top-class grade. In the highest categories, the remarkable Grace strain died as abruptly as it had arrived. It is obvious that, naturally enough, they had the pick of coaching and of opportunities, but to little notable avail. It was in the nature of things that W. G. Grace should risk a substantial emotional investment in his heir, the son who carried in his turn sport's most easily identifiable initials. The burden may well have been unsupportable.

How daunting it must have been to have W. G. Grace for a father! It was not that he was cruel or oppressive; far from it, he was strongly and affectionately attached to his children. But he was a jubilantly successful father in his own field of cricket, impossible to emulate, not only because he was inexorably efficient at the game but because he was also its modern progenitor. Besides that, he was always a little larger-than-life in his reactions. He must have found the balance of parenthood—that subtle awareness of when to steal quietly away and sympathise in silence—a difficult one to achieve. His insistent, clamouring encouragement may, at times, have been as disconcerting, even as wounding, as another's aloofness.

The persistent training from babyhood and the intense desire to mould another generation of cricketers was reminiscent of W.G.'s own father's, in his case, successful treatment. This time round the recipe did not come up to expectations. Bernard Darwin has said how W.G. was 'desperately and pathetically anxious' about his son's Blue, and there is something a little pitiful in his blinkered, optimistic determination that here was a chip off the old block. Grace was too overtly

and boisterously pleased at any minor success on W.G. Junior's part;
each such achievement fanned rather than dampened the flames of
paternal ambition. To score 40 for Cambridge at Lord's must, of
course, have pleased the young man immensely and the happiness it
gave his father must have pleased him—but a part of him must have
uneasily realised that such an act fed his father's vaunting aspiration.

All things are relative. A couple of Blues, a fifty at Lord's and a few
games with the county would, for thousands, comprise that crowded
hour of glorious life which Walter Scott felt was like an age without a
name. For W. G. Grace's chosen son, it was close to abject failure. In
the circumstances it might have been advisable to have selected
another arena of development for W.G. Junior, or to have allowed
him some choice in the matter. Stiff and ungainly, his batting was very
much of a mechanical, 'coached' character, and someone should have
recalled his Uncle Alfred who, although a pugnaciously useful club
cricketer, refused to be drawn into the brotherly competition. He
decided early on that horses were more predictable company than
cricketers, and he lived to a benign and interesting ripe old age in
Chipping Sodbury.

William Gilbert the younger was a withdrawn youth, and it is not
easy to decide where in the circle of cause and effect that reticence
occurred, whether in reaction to the pressure of a powerful Victorian
father or whether a natural diffidence made it hard for him to succeed
as a cricketing heir apparent. This is not to suggest there was any
severe psychological damage. The two W.G.'s never had a scarred or
broken relationship; many would prefer the younger's studious shy-
ness to the elder's brashness and the story is only unfamiliar in that it
took place in public.

What is most curious is that W.G.'s ambition for his sons was static
and immovable, an exact replica of their grandfather's hopes for himself. That dualism of great national cricketer and small-time country
doctor was his set image. He was as uncomprehending of his sons'
desire to adopt a different vocation as he was disappointed by their
comparative lack of sporting success. He apparently could not under-
stand why they had no wish to be parish doctors, presumably sporting
the same line that he did in baggy trousers, dark swallow-coat and
square felt hat, tramping or cycling from patient to patient in a semi-
rural practice. The fact that W.G. Junior went up to Pembroke
College and became a public-school master and that, in his turn, his
second son, Edgar, had a highly successful naval career, seemed
slightly to bemuse him.

Some of that, however, lay in the future. At this time, the early 1890s, Grace had the problems, it is true, of a growing family, but he was also plagued by cricketing questions, both technical and administrative. His recurring knee injury was a perpetual irritant, and, although the dearth of runs of 1891 was not quite repeated, 1892, 1893 and 1894 were poor years for him. In 1892 he doubled his 1891 total with an aggregate of over 800 runs, but, once more, he never scored a century, although he made a fine 99 against Sussex. The summer of 1893 was blessed with Grace's first century for three years—126 for MCC against Kent, and he averaged 30, his best for some years. In 1894, when he just failed with 1,293 runs to average 30, he reached three figures twice, against Cambridge, and then with 131 for the Gentlemen versus the Players at Hastings. That was his 98th century. It had taken him since 1888, when he scored his 89th century, to stumble through the 90s.

Grace with problems meant Gloucestershire with problems: the county was either bottom or not far from it during this period. Grace dropped down the order on occasion, and, in 1891, E. M. Grace, with 15, was second in the county averages to his younger brother, testimony to the team's impoverished batting.

It is, as Jane Austen might have said, 'a truth universally acknowledged' that when a sports team is on the slide, it is the popular idol who frequently takes the blame. Whatever the critical feelings about Grace bottled up during the years of his purple patches, it was only when he appeared as vulnerable and less than godlike that there was open carping.

The Gloucester professionals were weak in quantity and quality. In 1890 W. Murch and J. Stinchcombe had been signed, and they eked out their tiny wages by working for the County Ground Company for 6d an hour. Murch, despite Grace's favourable opinions, did little over several seasons, while, conversely, his judgement was considered faulty in allowing Nichol to move, with some success, to Somerset, and in not signing Kinneir, who went to Warwickshire where he opened the batting steadfastly for many years. Jack Board was engaged in 1890, and his first big game had been when, rushed to Lord's on the strength of a telegram from W.G. and of £2 hurriedly scrabbled from Mrs Grace's purse at Stapleton Road, he had kept wicket for the South versus the North. He was one of the few reasonably competent professionals contracted about this time.

The Champion preferred a preponderantly amateur team. 'There is another thing I am afraid of', he said, around this time, 'that is, that cricket will be made too much of a business, like football, with the consequence that none but professionals will be seen playing.' Were that to happen, 'Betting and all kindred evils will follow in its wake, and instead of the game being followed up for love, it will simply be a matter of £ s d.'

Grace's historical grasp had gone awry. It had been the amateur lordlings who had been responsible for the gambling in the past, and, as he should have recognised, the day of the dominant professional had also declined with the collapse of the exhibition XIs and the rationalisation of the county championship. At a personal level, and although Grace could not be faulted as to his profound love for the game, the 'matter of £ s d' had always been a significant consideration for him.

The truth was that W.G. favoured not only a team of amateurs, but a team of public school and university tyros, ignoring the club cricketers in the Gloucestershire area. Grace well knew that, whatever the potential, it was the more likely to be developed on the beautiful school and college grounds with coaches such as H. H. Stephenson, James Lillywhite and W. A. Woof to din the rudiments into the unmoulded cricketing consciousness. Equally, he had a marked emotional preference for the suave young gentry from school and varsity. When teams are losing, the call for local talent is stridently heard, and Gloucestershire committee men and club cricketers raised their voices. In 1873, the Gloucester committee, by resolution, delegated to their, so far, only skipper an absolute right in matters of selection, and, with autocratic bluffness, team management had been conducted in that dictatorial manner for twenty years. What Grace had agreed at the age of twenty-five, he was unlikely to find fault with aged forty-four.

At an evidently tempestuous meeting on 9 December 1892, with the Graces out in force, Henry as well as Edward and W.G. being present, the 'Big Doctor' disgustedly resigned. He was asked to reconsider this, and the chairman, H. W. Beloe, also offered his resignation. Both eventually resumed their duties, but W.G. was in no mood for compromise. Asked 'whether, if it be the general wish of the Committee, Dr Grace would be prepared to concur in appointing a selection committee as a means of preventing any recurrence of the troubles'., Grace answered curtly that 'simply for the sake of our county cricket' he would captain the side, but, as for the selection committee, 'I will have nothing to do with it. I do not think it will help us to win matches or that it would work at all satisfactorily.'

The storm rumbled on, its clouds louring around the deceptively sunny front presented by the committee. At cricket dinners and meetings and in the local newspapers the controversy continued. The attack on dictatorship was even, bravely, sustained in Grace's own presence, and at one such dinner he so far departed from his customary habit as to deliver a brief, colourful and unreserved answer. George Bradbeer, one of the local club captains involved in this dispute, rallied his side of the battle lines, pointing out, in the columns of the press, that Gloucestershire had won only eight games in four years and a few more honest-to-goodness club cricketers in the XI was the required prescription. The resurgence of Grace, with a fresh recruitment of amateurs in support, saved the day temporarily, but Grace's departure from the county was only postponed by this brief and exciting interlude. The final split was to come as little surprise for those who had recognised how the friction had continued throughout the decade.

Grace's unease about professionals was reflected in his martinet-like treatment of them. He was brusque with them, and did not allow familiarity on their part. He could also be kind, however, and always remained an energetic contributor to their benefit matches. If he showed annoyance with that snorting frankness of his, he could also make amends. His short note of apology to the Gloucester stumper, Board, whom he had belligerently scolded on the field, is a minor classic: 'Dear Jack, we all miss 'em sometimes. You less than most of us.' Part of the hostility in the professional ranks must have stemmed from his ruthlessness as a player. At the Jubilee dinner (1897) he was, rather ashamedly, to tell how he had halted, with a battery of 6s a promising colt from pursuing his career, and Neville Cardus has written of another young 'pro' reduced to tears by the doctor's severity on his bowling. The year after his 'Indian Summer', there was what W.G. called 'an inopportune strike' of five professionals on the eve of the Oval Test match. In his reminiscences, Grace, writing testily of that occasion, remarked that 'many irritating statements of an absolutely false character were made with regard to prominent amateur cricketers'. That he was one of the most prominent and also one of the most irritated can scarcely be doubted.

This kind of disaffection and his devotion to the public-school and university product must, however, be judged in the context of the age, for it was an age socially more static and less volatile than the one in which Grace began to play first-class cricket. And it is most striking how precisely late Victorian and Edwardian cricket reflected society.

After the alarums of mid-century, England was not, until 1914, to suffer violent stress at home or from abroad. Against a slowly improving background of material well-being and imperial grandeur, what emerged was a more stable and apparent class division, and there was, not totally but to an extent not experienced before or since in our industrial society, a maintenance of such harmony. There was a balance of upper, middle and working classes. It was not that there was no enmity nor bitterness but, by and large, hostilities were, whilst not abandoned, at least submerged. There was a delicately poised harmony rather than conflict.

Britain had reached what has been called 'the high point of its capitalist career'. Well over three-quarters of its population were of the 'manual labour class', and there remained a distinct chasm between this large proletariat and what, in fact, was a relatively small bourgeois or middle class. In late Victorian times there were probably not much more than 200,000 families like the Graces, about a quarter with incomes of over £1,000 a year, with the remainder earning down to £300 or £400 a year. The gap is indicated in the simple fact that the labour aristocracy would have been earning at best, £100 to £200 a year. This middle class, possibly encompassing, with wives and children, a million or two souls, consisted of merchants, factory owners, doctors, architects, lawyers and engineers. They employed a million and a half servants, and their capacity to do so was, as much as income, a sign of their bourgeois status. The division was physical as well as social. In 1880 the average twelve-year-old, upper-class, public-school boy was 5 inches taller than the working class lad of like age.

In terms of the gentleman-player syndrome, it is important to note the minute nature of that middling layer, the 'lower middle class'. White-collar workers—bank and company clerks and the like—were few in number, surprisingly so given the commercial character of the nation. This meant, in terms of status, that the steps from working class to middle class were steep. Arguably, the climb was more arduous now that stability was the norm. In the frenetic turmoil of the Industrial *Revolution*, upward mobility had been, if not easy, then less overt. The social definitions had been, for a while, not so pronounced and the hierarchies not so clearly defined.

Cricket, like industry, had gone through its own forging fires. Small-scale entrepreneurs, like William Clarke or Alfred Shaw, had been mixed up with the efforts of the aristocracy and gentry to launch county teams. Then, as the heat lowered and the mould cooled and

**"THE FIFTIETH YEAR OF GRACE."**
NOT OUT.

Punch cartoon of 1898 celebrating W.G.'s fiftieth birthday

Portrait of W. G. Grace by unknown artist

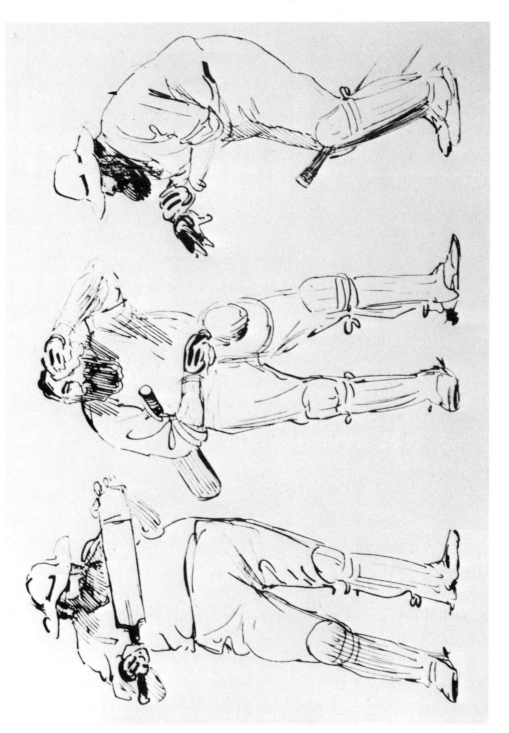

Three Harry Furniss cartoons of W.G., from *A Century of Grace*

W. G. Grace, aged approximately 60, and his wife at Ashley Grange

hardened, the division between the two categories of amateurs and professionals became more explicit. As in industry, the transformation in cricket was connected with its growth and its institutionalisation which reduced the possibilities for the small-time operator.

Jesse Boot, born in 1850, started in his father's herbalist shop at ten and by 1908 he owned several factories and 300 shops. Such chances of rising to riches or, conversely, bleak starvation remained, but both were now considerably lessened. As ever, cricket reflected this prevailing mood. Even the chance for small-time opportunists like Arthur Shrewsbury or Alfred Shaw to venture for profit overseas was just about finished. The game, at home and abroad, was absolutely in the control of a self-perpetuating establishment. The Jesse Boot of William Clarke became the Boots Limited of the MCC and the Imperial Cricket Conference. The cricket establishment gradually assumed a monopoly; it presumed to adopt the style and the statutory commitment of the royal chartered company of a century or so earlier.

The actual sport ruled over by the cabal of Marylebone was, of course, ideally suited to the static character of a dominant two-class system. It was, simply, a two-class game, with the pavilion (housing the county authorities and members) and the popular side standing proxy for the semi-detached bank manager's abode and the cotton-spinner's terraced house. Throughout the second half of the nineteenth century the actual architecture of many county grounds, with a much stricter distinction of place and the erection of the Gothic-like pavilion, underwent an overhaul of this kind. If it was not socially dividing, it was socially labelling, with, in turn, the treatment of professional as opposed to amateur—the separate gates and dressing rooms, the careful prefix of 'mister' and initials for amateurs as against the severe, plain surname for professionals—in parallel.

But cricket was so appropriate to the age because, crucially, professional and amateur played *together* and jointly entertained both classes from which they sprang. In that well-harmonised age perhaps the nearest other example of the integrated cult is the Gilbert and Sullivan convention. It enjoyed much the same heyday as cricket, (the Mikado was first produced in 1885) and, in W. S. Gilbert's own cheerful phrase, it provided both 'rump steak for the gallery and oyster sauce for the stalls'. Possibly the best illustration lies in the highly effective batting partnership, such as that of MacLaren and Tyldesley. Archie MacLaren was the epitome of the aristocratic style, and he had that strange mélange of strident dash and pessimistic phlegm which betokened the Edwardian toff. Tall and imperious at the crease, he was ably supported by his faithful lieutenant, J. T. Tyldesley. That powerfully built Lancastrian was his captain's equal in superb strokeplay. Each could match the other for skill and each developed a vividly personalised style, yet the social gulf between them remained immense.

Not that the lot of the average professional was so poor by the turn of the century. During the last quarter of the century the wages of the good-class professional rose from about £100 (made up of £4 or £5 match fee and bonuses) to £250 (by this time not match pay but more usually a contractual wage). This, of course, was the reward for a few months' work. Many cricketers had a winter job and a few would enjoy an overseas tour. Then there was the chance of a benefit—in 1904 Yorkshire's G. H. Hirst obtained £3,700 from the Lancashire match. By contrast the average labourer's yearly income rose from £80 to £100 over the same quarter century. The successful professional was in the upper echelon of the proletariat. He had, as like as not, escaped from mill or mine, and enjoyed the respect his more leisurely pursuit earned him in the eyes of his late fellows.

That was the brighter side. As with most professional sports, many were called but few were chosen. There were many unfortunates who either did not make the grade or who, having made the grade, declined into extreme poverty, that other hazard for the professional sportsman. Players who were in and out of sides and dependent on match fees might find life precarious and there were several forced to live rough and economise on cricket kit and clothing. As early as the 1860s a Cricketer's Fund had been formed, while county aristocrats such as Lord Hawke worked strenuously to protect the livelihood of professionals. The characteristic nineteenth-century vice of drunkenness was one which affected cricketers all too frequently to add to the risks. The game itself lends to social drinking and, with many of their colleagues themselves publicans, it was not surprising that alcoholism took its toll. There were likely to be those fans ever ready to buy the pints and boast thereafter of drinking with this or that famed cricketer, and this was a time when yet another professional-amateur distinction was that no meals were provided for the former but only for the latter.

The outer edges of cricket's class divisions, then, were well distanced. The wrecked, drink-sodden ex-professional, stumbling toward the workhouse door, was far removed from the wealth and lineage of cricket's upper crust. Consider the county presidents of about the 1880 period, a veritable dip into Debrett. Lord Enfield was president of Middlesex, and Lord Monson of Surrey, with the Prince of Wales as patron. Nottinghamshire fielded the Duke of St Albans, Gloucester the Duke of Beaufort (with Lord FitzHarding as vice-president) and Kent the Marquis of Abergavenny (with the Duke of Edinburgh as patron). The Earl of Sheffield was president of Sussex and the Earl of Cork and Orrery was president of Somerset. In 1881, and apart from HRH the Prince of Wales being its patron, the MCC had Lord George Hamilton as president, with five other lords and three honourables on the committee.

With undergraduates and public-school masters free over long summer vacations to swell the ranks of the gainfully unemployed, it is unlikely that, in the thirty years before the 1914-18 war, there were more than a hundred or so professionals making anything like a decent living, and only a Sydney Barnes could have the temerity and talent gruffly to take a stand. In effect, the systematic establishment of the county circuit was tantamount to the formation of a cartel, which rigidly controlled the provision of labour.

There was also the tendency for the paid to bowl and the unpaid to bat. Year after year—with Grace always the exception—professionals topped the bowling averages for more or less every county, while amateurs often headed the batting averages. The batting was not so exclusive a preserve as bowling. Tom Hayward, of Surrey, for example, became, in 1913, the second cricketer after Grace to reach a hundred hundreds. But until the time the amateur-professional distinction was abolished, no English amateur—apart from the dubious case of W.G. himself, who took nearly 3,000—had taken over 2,000 wickets.

In this, as in other aspects, Grace was the rule-proving exception. Otherwise the MacLaren-Tyldesley syndrome was dominant. The theme of master and servant facing common challenge or undertaking common duties in structured, disciplined style may be seen elsewhere in Victorian and Edwardian life. Two examples are obvious enough. One is the officer-non-commissioned officer relationship; the other the master-butler relationship. The senior professional was very much the regimental sergeant major, often much more orthodox in approach than his captain, and, like the butler, more alert to breaches of protocol. This trait was well illustrated in J. M. Barrie's play *The Admirable Crichton*, where, when the family are shipwrecked on a desert island; the butler's authority is open and not, as before and after the sojourn, covert.

Grace managed to close that gap between 'upstairs' and 'downstairs'. In status and family background, he came low in the echelons of the well-to-do, and was thus forced to pick out a salary for playing cricket when most of the others were either unpaid or wage-earners. Grace was getting older and closer to the establishment as cricket was, in class terms, becoming more rigid and more self-conscious. In that sense, he grew further away from the professional cadres. Even for so boisterous and seemingly insensitive a personality as his, some of the resentments and criticisms must have pierced his psychological defences. Certainly there is an over-reaction in his attack on the 'kindred evils' of cricket as a business, and upon those who might have regarded themselves as his fellow-professionals. Ranjitsinhji was foremost among the majority who realised that county cricket offered 'cheap, wholesome and desirable entertainment' to many people and that county teams, in so far as they had to be run on, literally, 'spectacular lines', required reliable craftsmen who could devote all their time to the game.

The views of Grace might have been passé and his actions occasionally questionable, but his sheer cricketing ingenuity and zeal forced everyone, establishment and populace, to tolerate and admire him. In a class, as opposed to a caste, system, society is, thankfully, ever vulnerable to the nonpareil, the out-and-out genius who transcends the conventions and flouts the social categories. This W. G. Grace was, and in no year was this more evident than in 1895, the season of his celebrated 'Indian Summer'.

The ailments to his legs had cleared, the Gloucester XI looked as if it might be less spineless than of yore, and a bright, cool spring permitted several weeks of long and valuable practice. His mental edge was obviously sharp, he was astoundingly fit for a man but a month away from his forty-eighth birthday and 101 against twenty-four Gloucestershire colts was his way of preparing for the battles before him. His first major game was at Lord's in the second week of May, for MCC against Sussex. Ranji made 150 before Grace deceived him, like so many lesser mortals before him, with the rustic simplicity of his first ball. Grace, caught by Ranji brilliantly for 13 in his first innings, scored 103 in the second, and this was his ninety-ninth century.

He scored only 18 and 25 for MCC against Yorkshire at Lord's, before moving down to Bristol for the Whitsuntide fixture with Somerset, comparative newcomers to the first-class ranks. The visitors batted first and batted well, their openers taking the score past 200, but, with Grace taking five wickets for 87, bowling as craftily as ever, they degenerated to 303 all out. Gloucester were soon in trouble, at 15 for 2, when C. L. Townsend, probably Grace's most scintillating protégé, joined his mentor. Townsend was to become one of the county's most famous players, renowned for his exciting batting and tidy spin-bowling, but he was, in 1895, a nervous Clifton schoolboy of eighteen. It was a novelettish situation: the shy, thin pupil and the ageing, hefty master routing the confident opposition. Grace was in absolute command, scoring with skill and assurance. When he was 98 the scorer signalled to Sam Woods, the Somerset fast bowler, and, with both bowler and batsman in some state of nerves, Woods lobbed a full toss for W.G. to dispatch to the leg-side boundary.

Grace became, in so doing, the first man ever to score a hundred first-class hundreds, and it is worth recalling that only one of them had been scored outside Britain. Of the eighteen players with a 'ton of tons' to their proud name, only nine have scored a hundred hundreds at home. The sad part of the proceedings was the smallness of the crowd, but the few gathered there tried to make the welkin ring, and, a pleasing thought, Agnes Grace and Bessie were present for that historic occasion.

To the chagrin of the Somerset bowlers, W.G. batted on with a god-like air of supremacy and, scoring at a rate of 55 an hour, he soon reached a second hundred. A magnum of champagne was ceremoniously carried forth on a tray and W.G. toasted himself at the wicket. Young Charles Townsend just failed to reach his first first-class hundred, leg before for 95, while Grace continued for five and a half hours in all until he was caught off the persevering Woods for 288. Gloucester's 474 was followed by a Somerset collapse which left the home side needing just a handful of runs for a nine-wicket victory.

It was a strange day. It opened in glaring spring sunshine, but later turned bitingly chilly. It was the day there were snowflakes in the Champion's thick beard, but apparently, nothing was to distract him. He never played a false shot and never gave a chance. The local Bristol paper said 'His cuts, square and late, were perfect, the ball travelling over the close-cut turf and reaching the boundary before the most agile of fielders had a chance to intervene; his drives were vigorous and safe, and his fours followed fast upon each other.'

It was as near perfect as a cricket innings can be. The Prebendary A. P. Wickham was Somerset's wicket-keeper and it was his careful recollection that, in five and a half hours, Grace 'only allowed four balls to pass him'. There were certainly only four byes in that Gloucestershire total but, if correct or anything like correct, Wickham's testimony demonstrates the eagerness and keenness of eye of the forty-seven-year-old doctor.

There was now no stopping Grace, as, brimming with self-assurance, he trod a regal, free-scoring pathway. After 52 for an England XI versus Cambridge University, he rejoined his county to play Kent at Gravesend. Kent amassed 470, but Grace was not to be intimidated. With just perhaps the ghost of a chance, he batted a little over seven hours and was last out for 257. Jack Painter, one of the professionals Grace constantly underbowled, suddenly blossomed in Kent's second innings and took seven wickets, leaving Gloucestershire 75 minutes to acquire the 103 necessary for a win. Grace led the charge. He was 73 not out at the end, and the 103 were scored in barely an hour. Grace fielded the first ball of the match; hit the last one for the winning runs; was never off the field for the duration of all four innings. The Gloucestershire XI were, for the first time ever, rapturously received by a big crowd around midnight when they arrived at Bristol station.

A few days passed before Grace was in action again, and this time he disappointed a huge Oval crowd when Tom Richardson bowled him for 18 in W. W. Read's benefit match, and, with Surrey collapsing, England had no need to bat a second time. He still required 153 runs to be the first man to score a thousand runs in May; indeed, the concept had never really been considered, such was the originality of the doctor's latest performances. There was just one chance. Gloucester played Middlesex at Lord's, and the game opened on 30 May. Fortunately, W.G. won the toss and batted. He was in subdued mood against a varied attack, including J. T. Hearne, and he managed but 58 between noon and the 2 pm luncheon interval. After lunch he obviously decided that submissiveness was neither his natural leaning nor the appropriate tactics. He drove and placed with consummate power, until, with a turned single on the leg-side, he reached his hundred. One problem was the disappearance into the Lord's pavilion of one partner after another, but A. J. Dearlove, a Bristol player, put up a stubborn defence. When Grace was 149 E. A. Nepean, the Middlesex slow bowler, delivered a long hop on the legside, and away it flashed to the boundary. A thousand runs in May: indeed in the twenty-two days since 9 May: it was the first time this had been achieved, and it had taken merely seven games and ten innings. Only Walter Hammond and Charlie Hallows have since managed that feat, as opposed to four others, Bradman twice, who had runs in April to contribute to their 1,000 runs before the end of May.

Having scored 169 against Middlesex, W.G. journeyed to Brighton, and scored 91 against Sussex. It was a changeable summer, with heavy rain in June and July, and Grace's batting suffered accordingly. In August fine weather and form were rediscovered in tandem, and he had scores of 119 against Nottinghamshire at Cheltenham; 118 out of 241 for the Gentlemen, his first against the Players at Lord's since 1876; 125 for MCC versus Kent at Lord's; 104 for South against North at Hastings; and 101 not out for the Gentlemen of England against I. Zingari, one of his five centuries that season at Lord's. Nine centuries in all. It was a sedate and uninterrupted processional of a summer for the middle-aged country doctor, and, although MacLaren just pipped him at the top of the averages, his aggregate of 2,346 runs was many more than anyone else's that year. The tall and promising tyro, Charles Townsend, took over a hundred wickets, and Gloucestershire, winning eight and losing six, sprang to fourth place in the table.

It was nineteen seasons since those heady days in the springtime of his career when he had scored 344 for MCC against Kent and 318 for Gloucester against Yorkshire. He had then been twenty-eight years old. The last few seasons had not seen him at anything like his most superlatively efficient, but, in 1895, he seemed to shrug off problems and metaphorically square his shoulders, and his daemonic energy did the rest. It was as if, conscious that time takes its toll of even the most obstinate constitutions, he rallied all his resources of physique and character for a final sublime 'Indian Summer'. He was for many more years to excel as a relentlessly effective batsman, but, in 1895, there was an almost metaphysical flavour to the perfection, to the matchless avoidance of error and of falseness of stroke play, at which he consistently aimed and frequently achieved. He transcended the petty distinctions between amateurs and professionals, and ascended above considerations of social and financial status.

# 11
# *W. G. Grace to the Leaving of Gloucestershire* (1895-9)

Public opinion erupted grandiloquently. It had slumbered for years during Grace's leaner phase, but his exploits now stirred up uncritical hero-worship in one of the first great national acclamations of a sporting star. Part ashamed of its earlier forgetfulness, part astounded at such exploits by, in terms of sport, a grizzled veteran, part stimulated by the ornate plaudits of the popular press, the British populace venerated and adored Grace with religious zeal.

Everyone from the Balloon Society of Great Britain—a medal for efficiently promoting 'the healthy development and preservation of the characteristics of active Englishmen'—to the Prince of Wales— 'his hearty congratulations upon this magnificent performance'— made clear their appreciation. This was the first time cricket had been royally complimented in this manner, 'official recognition' that such deeds were 'as worthy of such great public recognition' as those more solemn exploits normally supposed to catch royalty's elevated eye.

As the *Pall Mall Gazette* put it: 'He has drained the language of eulogy and it is no use applying superlatives to him any more.' Certainly the press seemed limitless in its adulation. Grace, 'the embodiment of courage, muscle and nerve, is a national glory'. To grant him a knighthood would satiate 'the universal desire of millions', and the government was told to go to the country on that grave issue. *Punch*, which found in Grace practically every physical and mental attribute it required for its sub-Dickensian caricatures, suggested he should become 'Companion of the Bat' and 'Cricket Field Marshal'. *Truth* lived up, in many minds, to its title by pointing out that Grace deserved the accolade far more than those who earned it through 'hours of obsequious begging'.

Whether it was conscience money for those few years of neglect or whether the urge to feel materially associated with this wave of at times near hysterical encomium, the public responded nobly. The deity worshipped, the offertory plates next had to be passed, with *The Daily Telegraph* as sidesman. That newspaper launched a popular 'National Shilling Testimonial' which raised over £4,000, including a fiver from the prime minister, Lord Salisbury, a token he pleasantly described as 'a centenary of shillings'.

Sir Edward Lawson, the proprietor of *The Daily Telegraph* and later, to become a press baron, as Lord Burnham, wrote a fulsome letter to W. G. Grace along with that handsome cheque. It was a hymn to the wholesome qualities of cricket, 'free from any element of cruelty, greed or coarseness'. Lawson felt the unquestioned success of his appeal was 'a manifestation by classes and masses alike of their abiding preference for wholesome and honest amusements in contradistinction to sickly pleasures and puritanical gloom'. A shrewd cartoon at the time showed W.G. thanking Sir Edward Lawson, who is saying, 'Don't mention it, doctor, look what you've done for my circulation.'

Two other funds, neither of them quite so productive, were raised. One was a combine of the *Sportsman* journal and the MCC, which raised well over £3,000, and the other a Gloucestershire appeal, under the auspices of the Duke of Beaufort, who was still president of the club. This raised about £1,500, the club itself donating £100, not a desperately large sum in view of Grace's endeavours on its behalf which, if only temporarily, had raised the county to the top of the championship table in June of 1895. But all in all, the triple testimonials scooped over £9,000 together, an extremely valuable perquisite to the income of a family man valiantly trying to educate four young people and establish them in careers. Excepting the entrepreneurial professionals such as Clarke, Lillywhite, Wisden, Parr, Shaw and Shrewsbury, it is doubtful whether many professionals of that time earned £9,000 in their entire career.

Then there were the by-products. A host of memorial souvenirs were produced and sold, chief among them the coveted plate, with each century recorded like spokes from the hub of Grace's imposing likeness. It was the fashion, and one greatly accentuated by the thousand runs in May and the hundredth century, to represent Grace, one of the most easily identifiable of Victorian heroes, in all kind of saleable items of crockery and linen. Whether and in what amounts,

W.G. obtained money by endorsements of these is questionable, but, certainly, the country, at commercial as well as journalistic, sporting and social levels, buzzed and echoed with his doings.

J. W. Arrowsmith, the organiser of several such events in the Gloucestershire calendar, arranged in an 'admirable manner' a 'Century of Centuries Banquet' on 24 June at the Victoria Rooms, Clifton, and festivities continued undiluted. C. L. R. James has posed the rhetorical question: 'On what other occasion, sporting or non-sporting, was there ever such enthusiasm, such an unforced sense of community, of the universal merged in an individual?' He was, argued James, 'strong with the strength of men who are filling a social need'. Encouraged by the realities both of his unprecedented batting attainment and its satisfying material rewards, W.G. turned toward the remaining handful of the century's seasons with restored exuberance.

The mundane daily round seemed unchanging and unchangeable. There was the doctoring, with the cycling now playing its part; the sacrosanct evenings at whist; even the muddy and exhausting pursuit of the beagles; the conventional but by no means, for the time, oppressive domestic life at Ashley Grange, the occasional social outings, with, unsurprisingly, the ebullient Grace finding the hectic flourishes of the polka his favourite form of dancing; and, of course, from late February through to the autumn, the interminable cricket. W.G. Junior graduated, and, doubtless aided by his famous name as well as his Cambridge degree, he quickly obtained a post as school master at Oundle. Henry Edgar, now aged eighteen, was embarking on his naval career, and the third son, Charles Butler, was following in his brother's footsteps at Clifton. But the Grace family, although settled foursquare, could not escape domestic tragedy. In the November of 1895, just after the glories of that summer and just at the time W.G. was in receipt of his generous testimonials, Dr Henry Grace died of apoplexy. He was sixty-three, no great age for an active medical man, who, while never of the first rank as a cricketer, had been a useful batsman and medium-paced bowler. More than that, he had replaced old Henry Grace as head of the family and had been something of a guide to W.G., particularly in his early years when an elder brother, some fifteen years separating them, was a decided asset. It had been his determination which led to W.G. playing a second and triumphant game for the MCC, all those years before in 1864, when he played those innings which thrust him over the threshold of first-class cricket. A close-knit family agonises that much more over its losses, and Henry Grace, as father figure, highly proficient doctor and Gloucestershire committee man, was to be profoundly missed. One wonders whether, had he survived a year or so, his stabilising quality might have prevented or, at least, rendered less painful, his younger brother's departure from Gloucester's fold.

Nonetheless, the death only two years later of Bessie Grace was doubly intolerable to Grace and his wife and family. Just before Christmas 1898 she contracted typhoid, and the fever carried her off with shattering abruptness. The Graces were stunned with grief. Everything that could be was unexpected about her untimely death. She had survived those early childhood years which were often so fatal in Victorian families and was in the first flush of maturity, just a few months beyond her twentieth birthday. The stresses of childbirth which as often then led to premature death among Victorian women were still before her; in fact, twenty was just about the healthiest age for a nineteenth-century female to be. She was outgoing, cheerful and affectionate, and much-loved. She shared the family interest in cricket; had played the game with some competence within the limited scope permitted the Victorian young lady and been deemed efficient enough to act as scorer for the Gloucestershire county XI.

A month later Grace was to leave his medical practice in Bristol, yield up his Gloucestershire captaincy and move to London in search of new leases on his life and his career. There were concrete reasons why both these affairs, medical and sporting, came to a head in 1899. It is difficult not to believe, however, and with some sympathy, that W.G. and Agnes Grace were thankful to leave the house and surrounds where their only daughter and favourite child had lived and died.

In the meanwhile, Grace had three full seasons more to play for Gloucestershire. The county seemed to have engineered a passage through its transitional period. The original side, built around the Graces, had gone; there had been an indifferent phase which had so roused the ire of Mr Bradbeer and his ilk; now the team was flourishing once more. This meant that Grace had no longer to shoulder the burden alone—not that he ever flinched from that role, but now the all-round performance of the county was improved. Charles Townsend was one of the most successful of the fresh recruits. The high action of his unusual and often lethal leg-breaks—he took 148 wickets in 1898—and his prolific record as a left-hand bat—he scored 2,440 runs the following year—made him one of England's leading all-rounders and gained him a Test place. Gilbert Jessop, twenty-one in

Grace's 'Indian Summer', was soon to add laurels for Gloucestershire to a choice career started at Cambridge University. The prototype hitter averaged in his best days 80 runs an hour: his longest ever innings—286 for the county versus Sussex in 1903—took him less than three hours, while, against the 1900 West Indians, he bewilderingly raced to 157 between 3.30 and 4.30 in the afternoon. To his sensational and incalculable onslaughts were added his adept pace bowling and his repute as one of the finest ever cover fielders. As well as these two young men, there were some lesser but brightish stars, one or two of them, like Jessop and W. G. Grace Junior, Cambridge Blues. The accent on the amateur was heavily emphasised, with Gloucestershire usually appearing with no more than a couple of professionals, normally at this time, Harry Wrathall and Jack Board.

Grace himself began 1896 as if there had been no winter. Once again the twenty-two young colts of Gloucestershire provided the aperitif; despite their youthful energies, the result was the same as in 1895, with W.G. scoring 108. Then the county played Sussex over the Whit weekend at Brighton, one of Grace's favoured grounds. He batted through the innings for an incredible 243 not out, and when, on a beautiful August Bank Holiday, Sussex made the journey to Bristol, Grace was ninth out with 301 (his third highest score) to his name. Although he never quite maintained that tempo, and scored only two other centuries, he ended the season with 2,135 runs, a first-class average of 42, making him fifth in the national averages.

The following season W.G. scored 1,500 runs, but kept his average well up, just falling short of the 40 mark. He scored four centuries, all for Gloucester, including one against the visiting Philadelphians, against whom he also took seven for 61. From tenth in the championship in 1896 to fifth in 1897 was a satisfactory improvement, while, in 1898, with Jessop and Townsend in excellent fettle, Gloucestershire proudly took third place in the county competition. Grace scored three centuries, all for Gloucestershire and all on opponents' grounds. It should have been four, and that at Bristol on August Bank Holiday before a huge crowd for the traditional Sussex match. To the spectators' disappointment, W.G., with eight wickets down and the match an obvious draw, suddenly declared at 93. This had a statistical explanation for 93 was Grace's only unnotched score en route from nil to a hundred, and he felt inclined to make it a clean sweep. That seems to give the lie to those who claim W.G. was not interested in figures.

Apart from leading his county in three of their most proficient seasons, Grace enjoyed, as ever, the opportunity to grapple with the Players and the Australians. With the exception of Grace, the Gentlemen were an extremely young team, and, although the professional batting was much improved, the amateur tended overall to maintain supremacy to the end of the century. Grace, with Stoddart, made a superlative opening partnership of 151 on a bad wicket in 1895 against the strong fast bowling of Richardson and Mold, and, in 1896 alongside sterling performances by Ranji and Stanley Jackson, the Cambridge and Yorkshire all-rounder, he led the Gentlemen to a fine six wickets victory.

In 1898 MCC arranged that the opening day of Gentlemen-Players fixture should coincide with the fiftieth birthday of the Champion. Good weather and bumper crowds made it a festive occasion. Both sides opened with scores of over 300, and W.G. chipped in with a sprightly 43. Left with 296 to get in three hours, Jack Hearne demolished the early amateur batting, but a dramatic stroke remained to add piquancy to a famous occasion. W.G., badly lamed and with a bruised and aching hand, batted low down in the order, and, with Kortright, the number eleven, he defended stoutly for almost ninety minutes in a brave attempt to save the match. Four minutes from time Charles Kortright was brilliantly caught, and the Players scraped home, with W.G. on 31, undefeated. A dinner was arranged and a special medal was struck to celebrate Grace's Jubilee Match.

Then there was the Australian challenge of 1899. Even in his doldrum years, W.G. had usually managed to whistle up a wind for the Australians: in 1893, for MCC and England, he had had six splendid opening stands with A. E. Stoddart, and England had won the series with a win and two draws rather in the home side's favour. The 1896 Australians, under Harry Trott, were of sterner mettle, with that formidable pair of left-handers, Joe Darling and Clem Hill, touring for the first time. England, under Grace, won two and lost one, that defeat despite an undefeated and masterly 154 from Ranjitsinhji and some determined bowling for thirteen wickets by Tom Richardson.

The rain-affected Test at the Oval, with wickets tumbling in all directions, was the infamous occasion when five of the professionals decided on strike action, with three eventually agreeing to play but Lohmann and Gunn remaining steadfastly intransigent. The professionals demanded vainly of the Surrey club, who, as was the practice, organised the match, that their fee of £10 should be doubled, and unkind words were breathed abroad about payments to amateurs. Such was the controversy, much of it directed at Grace, that C. W.

Alcock, the Surrey secretary, officially replied to press comments
with 'the most unqualified contradiction'. He stated that Surrey, over
many years, had always paid £10 to Grace for his expenses when he
was invited to play at the Oval and that 'beyond this amount Dr Grace
has not received, directly or indirectly, one farthing for playing at the
Oval'. It was a pity for C. W. Alcock that Grace's expenses and the
professionals' match fee was identical, and that a flat rate, irrespective
of commitments, was offered. Ten pounds was, of course, one month's
wages for many tradesmen at that time. Incidentally, Grace suffered
another bout of chagrin concerned with the Australians in 1896,
when, catching Gloucestershire on a sticky pitch at Cheltenham,
they ousted the county side for only 17 runs, Grace top-scoring with 9.

In 1899 the Australians returned under Darling's captaincy for the
first five-match series in England. W.G. played in the first test at
Nottingham, when, without fast-bowlers, England drew a game
largely dictated by the old enemy and saved only by Ranjitsinhji's
magic. Grace scored 20 and 8, and, a portly fifty-one year old, he
could not bend so agilely in the field. 'The ground's too far away', he
explained. He had long since moved to his brother Edward's fondest
position of point, and the days of his swift running in and sure arm
from the outfield were passed. At point his catching and picking up
were still amazingly good, but these skills could only be demonstrated
from a stationary position. There was some unkind jeering at Trent
Bridge and Grace, properly conscious of his own status and of the
standing of international cricket, made no fuss and quickly acquiesced
in his being dropped from the international side for the first time at
home in the history of such encounters. It was his unlucky thirteenth
outing as England's captain, and on C. B. Fry's vote, his place and the
captaincy was given to Archie MacLaren. He had played in twenty-
two tests, of which three had taken place in Australia. 'It's all over,
Jacker', Grace said, morosely but without rancour to Stanley
Jackson.

It was also all over apropos Gloucestershire during that same
season, 1899. W. Troup took charge of the county side in its trial
games, for instance, against the colts against whom Grace normally
made so merry. Grace joined the team for its southern safari through
Sussex, Kent, Surrey and Middlesex in the early days of May. On his
return home he was informed of a committee request for him to state
'exactly what matches he intends playing in for the county during the
year'. As he had thus far played in all Gloucester's first-class games,
the query might have appeared to some premature, but the committee

had learned that a London County Club was being established at the Crystal Palace and that W.G. had been invited to act as manager and skipper.

Grace's reply, from an address in Sydenham, was typically uncompromising and indeed offensive. Hinting at resolutions 'kept back from me for reasons best known to yourself' and at 'other actions of some of the committee', he claimed that he 'had intended to play in nearly all our matches', but, in the circumstances, 'I send in my resignation as captain, and must ask the Committee to choose the teams for future games, as I shall not get them up.' Getting them up is precisely what Grace had done for nearly thirty years. 'I shall need you', his selection letters peremptorily read, 'at Bristol against Notts., July 14, 15 and 16th.' It was a royal command. It was obvious that the troubles of the mid-1890s had rumbled on behind the scenes, and W.G. ended his letter to the committee with the ringing insult: 'I have the greatest affection for the county of my birth, but for the Committee as a body, the greatest contempt.'

This severe rebuke could hardly be countenanced by any 'self-respecting body', such as the county committee regarded itself, and they hoped at their meeting of 2 June, he would withdraw it. He would not and there was impasse. Conscious as they were of his past services, the committee felt 'deep regret at his severance from them in spite of the efforts which have been made by them to avoid it, but they felt they had no course open to them but to accept his resignation'.

In view of what one of his friendlier biographers has called 'his known peculiarity of temperament', the committee perhaps approached the matter in a tactless and ill-advised manner. W. G. Grace was not one to turn the other cheek and was decidedly touchy when faced with what he considered an affront. Conversely, it is evident that Grace was considering the London Club posts and it is difficult to see how he could have managed both. Truth to tell, many cricketers played for more than one team in the Victorian period, as Grace himself had earlier done for the United South and as he still did for MCC. Nonetheless, the county programme was now much fuller, as witness Gloucester's southern tour in the opening days of May 1899. Again, Grace was now fifty-one and unlikely to persist much longer as a regular player in the now very demanding county competition. It was, on any reckoning, a stiff contest, with the general standards of county cricket at an extremely high level. Perhaps the committee could have been a little less abrasive in its inquiries.

It is clear enough, however, that Grace would have wished to have undertaken the London as well as the Gloucestershire post, playing in, and the saving clause was critical, 'nearly all our matches'. In 1899 there had been some radical revisions and amalgamations in the Poor Law Unions in the Bristol area which, in Grace's opinion, adversely affected the parochial medical system with which he had been associated in Stapleton Road, since he qualified over twenty years before. In irritation and protest, he (along with other doctors) gave up his practice, and was thus anxious to find some remunerative activity.

Instinctively conservative in his ways and a creature who valued stability and continuity, Grace must have reeled under the three hammer-blows of a young daughter dead, a revamped medical service and a truculent committee. He moved to a new job at the Crystal Palace and a new home not too far away in south London. Grace had captained Gloucestershire since 1870, certainly the record period of service for a county captain in the history of the game. In 1899 he was in charge for the thirtieth consecutive season, a remarkable achievement. But given those thirty years of uninterrupted and unchallenged captaincy there is no gainsaying what a sore and biting wrench it must have been for the old warhorse. It was rather like the dictator of a one-party banana republic being displaced by a bloodless coup in favour of a tinpot military junta.

The analogy may be not too absurd. It is scarcely to be credited that the committee had in mind any other outcome. Rightly or wrongly, they cannot have embarked on so imperious an enterprise, with their lengthy acquaintance of W.G. and his tetchy reactions, without the consequences more or less predetermined in their minds. In brief, the committee most probably wanted to see Grace depart, the more so as his performance was now beginning to weigh less in the balance against his tyrannous behaviour. He went to London and managed the Crystal Palace ground and captained the London County XI, just as the committee knew he had been requested to do. He never scored a century in 1899, although he was run out when close to yet another hundred against the Players. He scored 78 out of a formidable 480, and the professionals succumbed again, in their first innings, to the lob-bowling of D. L. A. Jephson. Grace had not forgotten the Australians. For the MCC he scored a sound fifty against Darling's team, with Ernest Jones, as in 1896, bowling at his briskest—the man, incidentally, who traditionally is supposed to have bowled a bumper straight through the Doctor's whiskers.

One intriguing sideline on the clash between Gloucestershire and their famous skipper is the part played by E. M. Grace, who had been secretary, and an autocratic one at that, for as long as his brother had been captain. He retired, in fact, from that office in 1909, just short of forty years in the secretaryship, and the Duke of Beaufort presented him with £600 and a walking-stick in the Grand Hotel, Bristol, to mark his retirement. The admirable J. W. Arrowsmith was once more a moving spirit in the raising of that testimonial.

One biography has astutely drawn attention to the lack of reference to W.G.'s exploits in Gloucestershire's records under E.M.'s surveillance. Were W.G.'s life to be written using but that source, it would be, according to A. G. Powell and S. C. Caple, 'a very meagre one'. Generous-spirited, they account for this as 'a natural disinclination to extol the deeds of a member of his family'. Yet this diffidence might also have been caused by some frustration at a younger brother's enduring success and some not unnatural feeling that the younger man obtained too much of the limelight. It is not unknown for families as close as the Graces to harbour acrid rivalries among their kith and kin, and, in his youth, E.M. had been regarded as the coming maestro, only to be overtaken and overshadowed by the superiority of his brother. There were differences between them. Woof paid handsome tribute to E.M.'s kindly treatment of professionals, who 'was much liked by them', not least because he successfully campaigned for bowlers with six wickets in an innings to earn talent money as well as batsmen with 50 runs. Then he was adamant about amateur status. E.M. wrote, in 1908, 'In the old days *gentlemen* used to pay their own expenses, and not, as now, charge every penny out of pocket, and often-times more, to those that they play for.' As for the County Championship, upon which W.G. had been so influential as player and instigator, 'There ought never to have been one, and the sooner it is done away with the better. It simply spoils the pleasure of cricket.' This worship of 'profit and averages and expense' was, he felt, a great evil, and he yearned for the days when Gloucester played but four counties 'home and out', won most of them and enjoyed, if not overwhelming, then at least more enthusiastic public support than thirty or forty years later.

These were central issues on which W.G. clashed, certainly in his actions, with his older brother, who may have well, by 1899, lost patience with him. Put negatively, he apparently did little, in his doubly privileged position as the club's chief officer and head of the Grace clan, to heal the breach. He may even have enjoyed the fracas, in that masochistic way some enjoy a rough-house, verbal or otherwise. It has been said that he enjoyed arguments as much as cricket matches, and he was assuredly a wily and verbose curmudgeon.

Well though he played for the county, his chief affections and energies were devoted to his beloved Thornbury club. He played for Thornbury from 1870, two years after Gladstone became prime minister, to 1910, when Edward VII died, that is throughout the club's established history. For almost the whole of this period he was prime all-rounder and single-handed organiser, and, between 1872 and 1892, he scored over 22,000 runs and took over 2,400 wickets for Thornbury. Even when the team was loaded, as often it was, with county players, E.M. was in the van, and was notoriously possessive about his bowling. In 1902 the Somerset player, W. Hyman, hit him for thirty-two 6s and took 62 off him in two overs, whereat E.M. persisted with his bowling as 'he's beginning to nibble'. In 1904, aged 63, he took five for 320 against Newport. Apart from 1885, when he was injured, and 1908, when financial reasons prevented the club from operating, he bowled and battled on until he was almost sixty-nine, and his son, Edgar Mervyn Grace, a Cambridge graduate, Blue-less but a sound club cricketer, bought his father's practice and took over the organisation of the Thornbury club. The Graces' insistence on continuity in professional, domestic and sporting matters had again triumphed.

The tales that abound about E. M. Grace are as bizarre as those told about his more famous brother. True or false, they cast a light on the character in which the family were regarded: he used the 'two minute' rule to dismiss opponents; the Thornbury CC Committee never met for over twenty-five years; one morning he appealed, successfully, for leg before apropos the last ball of the preceding evening; as a coroner, he was the only one to hold a Sunday inquest, and that in order to join Lord FitzHarding's hunt; he caught a swallow at point, so quick were his reflexes; he had a corpse placed on ice until close of play; when, in astonishment, a visiting skipper ejaculated 'I declare' while batting, E.M. insisted on interpreting him literally. He ranged from the genial to the obstreperous, but was never quiet. 'If', said one ear-witness, 'W.G. were playing too you could hardly hear yourself speak.' During a lengthy disputation in a county match, a gallery wit cried 'Hold an inquest on it, coroner', and E. M. Grace caught the comedian and flung him out of the ground. He was an adept at winning the toss. One season he certainly won it thirty-eight out of forty times, ingenuously explaining that his eyes were efficient enough for him to watch the coin at the top of the spin and shout appropriately. However he managed it, moral rectitude never suggested to him that one is not supposed to try to win the toss.

To round off this aspect of the Grace legend, there came a time when E.M. could hardly bowl the length of the wicket and finally, in the summer of 1910, at Alveston, he had to be carried unconscious from the cricket field, having collapsed, exhausted. The following May, in his room overlooking the Severn, he died of a cerebral haemorrhage, six months short of his seventieth birthday. Gloucestershire were playing at Northampton, and, on receipt of the news, the players wore black mourning bands and the flags were lowered to half-mast. He was carried a few days later the twelve-mile trip from Thornbury, where he had raised his huge family, doctored the locality, and managed both county and club teams, back to Downend, where he was buried in the churchyard 'within a cricket-ball's throw of the spot where he gained his great love for the game of which he was so great an ornament'.

One forms the impression that the feelings between W. G. Grace and his elder brother, E. M., were decidedly ambivalent. When they were, in cricket or other matters, on the same side, their camaraderie was of the staunchest. They made a formidable combine. When, however, they were, as cricketers or on family or administrative issues, at all opposed to one another, there are signs that these filial links could be strained. It is likely that, in temper and character, they were too close for comfort and that on occasion the similarity of their personalities made for some unease.

# 12
# Grace at the Crystal Palace and after (1899-1915)

As Grace departed from the Test match arena and from Gloucester-shire, he might, had he been of a retrospective turn of mind, have thought back over thirty-five years in which cricket had become a national spectacle, with Grace himself its chief performer. Indeed, it is arguable that, as the major national sport, it did not really survive him, for football was about to overtake cricket in popularity. About 1890 the first-class cricket programme of a hundred matches was watched by some 2 million people, while the hundred or so Football League matches drew crowds which totalled about a million. 20,000 watched on that famous occasion in 1878 when the Australians first beat the MCC, and 20,000 was considered a normal attendance for a day of the Gentlemen and Players fixture or the then highly esteemed Varsity match. It was 1889 before the FA Cup Final attracted 20,000, when Preston North End beat Wolves 3-0—and that was at the Oval.

Several factors contributed to cricket's mass appeal. Population—and a population with more leisure—was obviously important: all the first-class counties were among England's most densely populated shires, and they tended to be based on populous towns: Gloucester-shire, for example, made its home in Bristol rather than the smaller county town. By the time Grace left the Bristol area, the city's population was 356,000: it had almost trebled itself in his lifetime and in the same period the port's annual tonnage of cargo had multiplied ten-fold. Clifton was heavily populated; Stapleton and Mangotsfield had been developed residentially and industrially; Kingswood and Hanham were noted for their footwear workshops.

By the time W. G. Grace gave up his practice, he could hardly still legitimately be called a country doctor.

Transport was another essential factor, and, without the country's mesh of railways, the first-class programme would have been unthinkable. With the amateurs travelling first-class and the professionals third-class, trains made all possible, and very soon the town without rail links could wave goodbye to first-class cricket. The building of Ashley Down Station near the Bristol ground, venue for many of W. G. Grace's exploits, is an illustration of this.

One element rebounds on another. Thus this web of rail communication, coupled with the growth of literacy and the abolition of the Stamp Tax on newspapers, enabled mass circulation dailies to reach thousands of ordinary people with their news of Grace and his confrères. It was in 1900 that the *Daily Mail* became the first English newspaper to reach a circulation of a million—and then there were the dozens of cricket manuals and periodicals as well as, from 1890 onwards, the celebrated cigarette cards.

W. G. Grace tells in his memoirs of a time when Lord's had gravel on its pitch, no shelter for the scorers and no fixed boundaries, apart from it being 4 to the pavilion rails. Spectators had once courteously parted to permit passage for the well-struck ball, but crowd pressures grew too great: turnstiles on cricket grounds and Bank Holidays arrived simultaneously in 1871. Grace dramatised the formal introduction of the boundary with the tale of A. N. Hornby dashing energetically into the crowd at Lord's and bowling over some old gentlemen who suffered grievous injuries. This led, according to Grace, to the wholesale adoption of boundary ropes or lines. Scoreboards, too, were added in response to spectator interest. W. G. Grace recounted the story of the fielder watching a long and, unbeknown to him, winning hit sail into what was aptly termed the 'country'. With a cry of 'back me up', he gave chase, turned, and to his dismay, everywhere was deserted, for everyone had retired to the pavilion. A scoreboard and a boundary picket would have saved him any such embarrassment.

And central to this widespread enthusiasm—including, as *Wisden* records, at least twelve games on ice, one by moonlight, during the severe 1879/80 winter—was the figure of Grace. It is said that the trains would await his pleasure as he completed his conversation, and adulation, in the late Victorian era, could go no further. It is immensely to his credit that, faced with such acclaim, he retained a bright spark of generosity and zest to the end of his career. Cheerfully egotistical as he was, Grace must surely have suffered some psychological scars.

Probably no sportsman, not even Pele or Arnold Palmer, has had to carry such responsibility for the very existence of his sport as a first-class spectacle. It had been Grace's task to prove cricket in the setting of its highest technical standards and in the attracting of its greatest number of spectators. That the public sometimes paid twice the normal admission fee if he were playing and that, as Clifford Bax wrote, 'It was rumoured that he would find a crinkling five pound note under his plate at luncheon' must only have increased the burden. Perhaps this sense of responsibility explains some of Grace's notoriously unsporting acts. There is the story of his running out from point an Australian innocently tending the pitch, an action which is said to have drawn both shouted rebuke and devastating revenge from Spofforth. Or there is the anecdote told of his refusal to be out, saying testily to the disgruntled bowler 'They've come here to watch me bat, not watch you bowl.' This could represent the authentic voice of a man taking an extremely business-like view of his position, for Grace well knew that he was the guarantor of cricket's popularity.

Still Grace was not one for regrets and retrospects. Not for him thoughts of an era completed and a passage of history negotiated as the century and the reign drew to a close. Rather did his mind turn to the London County Club and what might be accomplished there. His annual fee of £600 was most acceptable for a summer's work, and doubtless distracted his mind from any brooding over the wrongs done him by the Gloucestershire committee and the Bristol Poor Law Union.

He could certainly count his seasons of work for Gloucestershire with every satisfaction. His averages had ranged over his thirty-one years with the club from just below 20 in 1894 to just below 81 in 1876. In 568 completed innings over what must have seemed a lifetime he averaged just over 40, scoring over 23,000 runs for the county. Up to the end of the 1880s he sustained his skilful and effective bowling. For Gloucestershire he took 1,363 wickets at the cost of about 18 apiece. He scored no less than 53 centuries for Gloucestershire, one for every ten or eleven completed innings. One record which is probably unassailable is that he carried his bat through an innings on no less than 17 occasions, several of them for Gloucestershire. Twice for the MCC he had taken ten wickets in an innings: for 92 against Kent in 1873, and for 49 against Oxford in 1886. For twenty or so years as an all-rounder and for another ten years chiefly as a batsman, he maintained these heights of consistency and success.

Others may challenge him in terms of quality as the greatest all-rounder who ever lived. Only Wilfred Rhodes and Frank Woolley approach W.G. for maintenance of efficiency over so lengthy a period: he played in first-class cricket in forty-four consecutive seasons, twenty-five of them as an all-rounder.

W. G. Grace was also one of the first cricketers to turn author in order to augment his income. Like many another sportsman, he was heavily reliant on ghost writers. His biographer, Methven-Brownlee, was one, while William Yardley, Arthur Porritt and E. H. D. Sewell were others. *Cricket* had appeared in 1891 and *History of a Hundred Centuries* in 1895, and these were crowned in 1899 with the publication of *W.G.: Cricketing Reminiscences and Personal Recollections*. Published by James Bowden, it was far and away his most-read, perhaps best written book, and helped make 1899 one of the more eventful years of that crowded life. His fourth and last work, *W.G.'s Little Book*, came out in 1909.

In an illuminating chapter, 'Collaborating with Grace', in his book *The Best I Remember*, Arthur Porritt relates how he single-handedly came to write the *Reminiscences* and what a struggle it was. For twelve months he battled to save from extinction the contract to produce the manuscript, sometimes leaving Grace's house, which he visited thrice weekly, 'in absolute despair'. In a telling phrase, Porritt said he found W.G. 'a singularly inarticulate man', quite unable to explain his inner feelings while batting—'no time for feeling with the next ball to be faced', the author was severely told—or to analyse the intellectual process behind his astute captaincy. As with many another genius, cerebral examination of the reasons for success were quite beyond Grace, and Arthur Porritt had to bake what literary bricks he could with precious little straw. All this he found, like so many others, part-fascinating and part-frustrating. 'A wonderful kindliness ran through his nature', he wrote, 'mingling strangely with the arbitrary temper of a man who had been accustomed to be dominant over other men.'

Then there were his 'gusty' temper and the prejudices which 'ran away with him'. According to Porritt, his twin hatreds were radical politicians and umpires who gave him out lbw. As Gilbert Jessop said of fielding within earshot of W.G. 'I would lend respectful ears to the relation of the extraordinary ignorance prevalent in umpiring circles concerning the proper rendition of law 24.' For Grace the umpires were often wrong about lbw, whether he was batting or bowling.

But Porritt's most surprising revelation was the notion that Grace, most indefatigable and untiring of athletes, had only one lung. Indeed, Porritt's scepticism led to the stormiest of several raging scenes, and Agnes Grace was hauled in to corroborate this astonishing piece of medical history. He had had only one lung 'since childhood', an odd phrase, given the absence of major chest surgery in mid-nineteenth century, and perhaps W.G. was referring back to the serious effects of his teenage pneumonia. If true, and the Graces were, after all, a family of doctors, it makes his notable stamina even more amazing. If untrue, one can only wonder at a curious and unnecessary piece of self-deception. Incidentally, Porritt adds one of the neatest of the myriad Grace puns, given that the *Reminiscences* were serialised weekly in the *Echo*.

> Grace: 'tis a charming sound
> Harmonious to the ear
> Heaven with the echo shall resound
> And all the earth shall hear.

No centuries were forthcoming to bless that year of 1899. The rift with Gloucester and the end of Test cricket were serious fractures in W.G.'s career, and the London County Club was not granted first-class status in any matches until 1900. But it was a very busy year, even if the cricket was sporadic in quality and results. The Grace family moved to Eltham, in south-east London, and here they made their home after that long sojourn near Bristol. Married life for Agnes and her famous spouse began and ended in London. The three boys were, of course, grown up, with the youngest, Charles, just about finishing his schooling at Clifton. He played for the school XI in 1899.

One last domestic blow was to cudgel the Graces during their life at Eltham. In 1903 W.G. Junior had moved to the Royal Naval College, Osborne, as one of the teachers there, and seemed well set for an estimable career. Unluckily, in February 1905 he suffered an appendicitis, at that time a dangerous complaint which had all but dispatched Edward VII just before his coronation three years earlier. The child in whom W. G. Grace had bestowed so much hope for some kind of reincarnation of his own life and work died on 2 March at East Cowes. Like his sister Bessie, he appeared to have navigated the perils of childhood illness, only to be struck down in manhood, for he was in his thirty-first year. With his Cambridge Blues and his handful of county games, he had perhaps approached too closely his father's aspirations, so that his relative failure as a cricketer was a severer knock than had he shown no interest or capability at all. That August Bank Holiday in 1896 when, before a numerous and admiring concourse, father and son had opened together for Gloucestershire, the son to be abruptly dismissed for one, and the father, next day, to score 301 not out somehow encapsulated the relationship: the father finding life and cricket a simple, successful matter; the son striving awkwardly and vainly to emulate him. As *The Star* said in 1895, 'There was something pathetic about seeing old W.G. and young W.G. at the wicket together.'

The young man had done well enough in minor cricket. He had scored 148 not out for his father's XI at the Reigate Festival in 1894 and, while at Cambridge in 1896, he shared in a massive opening stand of 337—his share being 213—for Pembroke against Caius. In 1901 he joined Billy Murdoch in a first-wicket stand of 355 (he scored 150) for London County versus the aptly labelled Erratics, and took all ten wickets for the same team against Bromley Town. A week or so after his death, *Cricket* claimed he had not been given a fair trial by his university, which had over-reacted against possible charges of being too much influenced by the family escutcheon. Nonetheless, he was short-sighted (and his glasses sometimes afforded him little aid), he was stiff and he was overly methodical. Claude Buckingham, a cricket writer of the day, said in the same issue of *Cricket* that his style demonstrated 'a forced and unnatural response to the parent's coaching'. Although there were those, rather sycophantically, who spoke of a filial resemblance, this was probably a shrewder assessment. The other two Grace boys always maintained that their father coached them but little and, in general, he had a wholesome scepticism about a mechanistic approach to coaching. W.G. Junior was perhaps the exception: the child upon whom so heavy a burden was placed that both father and son tried too hard. It is sad to recall that, for the Varsity match in which his son played, Grace bought his first-ever silk hat and frockcoat, and it was the first first-class match at which he was a mere spectator.

Poor Bert (as the family knew him) did not even have the constitution or the good fortune to prove himself in some other sphere, such as school-mastering. Like so many parents in that age, Agnes and W. G. Grace had to share the grief and bear the shock of half their family torn away by death. Fortunately, and although neither were to become noted cricketers, the other two sons lived longer and conventionally successful lives. C. B. Grace lived, a well-qualified electrical engineer until 1938, dying at the age of fifty-six, in a manner his father might have prescribed, while making the winning hit in a club cricket match. H. E. Grace, a captain in 1914 and his prospects speeded by the expediencies of the Great War, rose to be a vice-admiral and a Companion of the Bath. He died in 1937, aged 61. Just one of Grace's nephews, Alfred, succeeded in being anything of a cricketer, playing for Epsom College and then some games for Gloucestershire during W.G.'s last years with the club.

Grace himself was over fifty when he returned to London. His eye was still chirpy and shining, and, for all his ponderous bulk, he retained unusual energy for outside sports. His inimitable trademark, the Old Testament beard, still hung, flat, shapeless and long, down his barrel of a chest. The despair of the manufacturers of shaving equipment, Grace never, so it has been said, stropped a razor in his life. In fact, there is some photographic and circumstantial evidence to suggest that, for a brief period around 1871 or 1872, Grace did make a few desultory passes at that luxuriant growth. But somehow the beard kept symbolic faith with the Grace story. Wispy and straggly as W.G. ventured, youthfully and hopefully, to establish his claim, it soon dropped from the cliff-edge of his jutting chin like a raven-black cataract as he stormed in triumph through the 1870s. Gradually, as he slowed a little, it mellowed, lightened in colour and was mottled with grey. Finally, in his later years, it hung, fully grey-white, like an outsize in Santa Claus disguises, many inches toward his rather gross waist. Although its pigmentation altered, its characteristic thickness was never enfeebled.

His eagerness for country sports never weakened either, despite the urbanisation of cricket and of his own life-style. His eye, steely and true, made him as accurate a shot as he was prolific a run-getter. Notably with his friend of later years, Herbert Gibbs, he ensured that feather and fur continued to fly in all directions until the end of his own life. Fish also had to be on their guard: he was a very keen angler, especially in the Trent. For so old and heavy a man, he also retained his taste for the beagles until late on in life, while, on moving to London, he began to play golf seriously and regularly rather than spasmodically. It is said that, given anything reasonably holeable, he would sink putts with equanimity, but that his iron shots up to the green were somewhat cavalier.

Not that he stuck to hunting and shooting, or even golfing. Interestingly, he adopted bowls, which had been widely taken up by town-dwellers, for its relatively confined arena was most suitable for the public parks and recreation grounds of urban districts. W.G. probably spotted that bowls was not always the peaceable and relaxing pastime that on the surface it appeared. It is, and can be, played with ferocious intensity, and W.G. entered into the company of bowlers with all the will and exuberance with which he tackled any chosen pursuit. He was inordinately proud of the smooth beauties of the Crystal Palace bowling green, and quickly became an adept, his finely tuned judgement of length giving him a decided advantage. He captained England in the first ever bowls international, against Scotland in 1903, and he was an England bowls player for the following five years as well. Indeed Grace has sometimes been labelled 'the Father of International Bowls'. Curling was yet another sport he enjoyed, whilst indoors his devotion to whist and long sessions of billiards was unremitting. He was also an occasional, never a persistent, gambler. The major omission to this life-long engagement with sporting diversions was lawn tennis, prominent since 1874 and with the first Wimbledon championship competed for as early as 1877. One might guess that the feminine association with tennis and its then mild air of effeteness would have been off-putting for W.G. He was very much a man's man in his choice of pastimes, and women, was his implied view, should be relegated to the kitchen and the dance-floor. The first Wimbledon women's championship was in 1884.

The hours he kept were mercilessly rural in character. Writing in 1921, Colonel Philip Trevor spoke feelingly of staying with the Graces, not long before W.G.'s death, and how unabated was the labour. Up at six with the gun, with shooting before and after breakfast; then off to the cricket, with net practice over lunch; then, just to keep the troops in trim, a route march back to the house, where, after dinner, there would be billiards until the small hours. In fact, after one or two days and nights of this tiring ritual, Grace was surprised when his younger colleagues begged for lights-out at midnight. Jessop found him a disappointing conversationalist, just as Porritt and many others did. 'You could rarely get him to talk about himself', a pleasingly modest but occasionally infuriating trait. But the reluctant talker was the relentless practitioner. Gilbert Jessop, Grace's protégé and his successor as the Gloucestershire skipper, goes on to record a typical day. When W.G. was sixty, Jessop accompanied him, through the most inclement weather, over no less than forty-five holes of golf at Maidenhead; then back to town for a hearty dinner, and on to the Prince's Ice-skating Club for Jessop to be introduced to the mystiques of curling, a process which took until after midnight.

Grace had been bred in a fairly Spartan country house and never became self-indulgent. His weight was something of a problem, and he endeavoured to eat sparingly and plainly. Plainness is a relative term: it was an age of lusty trenchermen, with Edward VII personally giving a lead to his subjects. The king liked to begin the day with haddock, poached eggs, bacon, chicken and woodcock for breakfast, as a comparatively sparse prelude to a twelve-course luncheon and a twelve-course dinner. The coronation banquet in 1902 had fourteen courses. However, Grace probably ate less than most of the preposterously greedy members of his own class and the upper class, and, unlike many of them, he was an habitual non-smoker. 'You can get rid of drink but not of smoke' was his characteristically terse and earthy aphorism. He drank moderately as well. While playing he would content himself with a single whisky and soda, with angostura bitters, at lunch-time, with possibly some more purposeful imbibing in the evening. Special occasions demanded champagne, and, once in a while, W.G. was not averse to swallowing champagne in quantity. Later in life, in order to slim, he drank cider, although latter-day dieticians might look askance at a GP supping scrumpy to reduce his waistline. Still, by the norms of the day, he did not come within a mile of living in luxury, let alone wallowing in dissipation. This care was obviously a factor in his capacity to play games for long hours over many years. Richard Daft concluded 'The two great secrets of his success have been his great self-denial and his constant practice.'

It was cricket and bowls he played at the Crystal Palace. The Crystal Palace itself was a kind of gigantic, baroque greenhouse, designed by the Duke of Devonshire's head gardener, Joseph Paxton, and erected in Hyde Park to house the Great Exhibition of 1851. In 1854 it was re-erected as the centrepiece of a sports and recreational complex at Penge, and, until the disastrous fire of 1936, was a celebrated landmark. Penge was only a mile or so from Grace's new home, and, over the next summers, his working life was circumscribed within that portion of south-east London.

The notion was that W.G. would help promote the Crystal Palace as a tourist haunt, for, it was believed, thousands would flock to view him at the wicket, rather as if he were a mounted sentry on Horse Guards Parade or a Beefeater at the Tower of London. After a few games in 1899, the newly formed London County Club, established in the wake of the formation of the London County Council in 1888, had certain of its matches recognised as first-class by the MCC, usually benign in its attitude to W.G.'s ventures. With their dark-green caps with red and yellow bands, they made a resplendent picture, and the guests on whom they chiefly relied were resplendent names. C. B. Fry and Charles Townsend were two, while the most regular was William Murdoch, the one-time Australian captain. Along with Ferris and Woods, he played for England as well as Australia, but all three played against South Africa—Billy Midwinter remains unique with his record of playing for Australia versus England and vice versa. Grace had made a firm friend of and enjoyed many boisterous times with Murdoch who acted as W.G.'s golfing partner many times. It was also as captain of London County that W.G. discovered Len Braund, the England and Somerset professional.

Over the seasons Grace added a few centuries to his collection. In 1900 he scored his last century at Lord's. It was 126 for the South versus the North. He then scored seven centuries at Crystal Palace over five seasons, four against MCC Club and Ground. He was still trundling away with the ball: in 1901 he had match figures of thirteen for 110 against MCC. In 1902 he played against Australia for the last time. His all-round performance for the Gentlemen was quite remarkable, for he scored 82 and took five for 29 against Darling's tourists, who included Victor Trumper and, some say, were the strongest touring side to visit these islands.

Unlike the Almighty, W.G. was quick to chide and, if slower to bless, he did not bear grudges. In 1903 the Gloucestershire committee resolved 'that in recognition of his services to the Gloucestershire County Cricket Club, Dr W. G. Grace be elected a life-member of the Club', and both Grace and his old committee colleagues were relieved and happy that their recent spat, which Jessop for one found quite incomprehensible, was finished and with dignity on both sides. That same season Gloucestershire visited the Crystal Palace and were lavishly received. The hospitality did not stretch to the cricket. Grace took six for 80 as his old county piled up a tall score. He then went on to score a 150, a friendly retribution if ever there were one. Gloucestershire collapsed the second time around, and London won by seven wickets. They won the return at Gloucester by five wickets. That was Grace's last first-class game in the county, although in 1908 he revisited Bristol for a final time when he played in John Spry's benefit match.

The dignified exits continued, and their dramatic content was seldom less than sparkling. In 1904 on his fifty-sixth birthday he scored his last century. It was against MCC, and it was his highest score, 166, since 1898. The same year he played his last match for

MCC, whose cap he had worn for so many seasons, faded and tiny on that craggy head. He scored 27 against the South Africans.

In 1905 the uneven and patchy experiment of playing first-class cricket at the Crystal Palace ended. It had not been economically viable. With so much first-class cricket already available in London, it was always a dubious proposition, and, like Kerry Packer seventy years later, the Crystal Palace authorities found that they had 'no partisan nucleus'. The cricket was cheery, often highly skilled, but it lacked the sharp competitive thrust which stems from identification with a particular locality.

Grace continued to play cricket, and, in 1906, there came his final major appearance, appropriately around his fifty-eighth birthday, and playing for the Gentlemen at the Oval. It was forty-one years since he had made his debut in that traditional fixture, and, over those years, he had scored over 6,000 runs and taken over 300 Players' wickets. He had scored fifteen centuries against the Players. Now by any sporting standards an ageing veteran, he scored a dogged 74, trudged back into the Oval dressing room, threw his bat down on the table, and declared, 'There. I shan't play any more.'

In the event, he played in a couple more first-class fixtures, both for the Gentlemen against Surrey at the Oval, both opening—and chilly—matches of the 1907 and 1908 seasons respectively. He scored 15 and 25 in the 1908 match, just a few weeks before his sixtieth birthday.

The Graces moved to Mottingham, to 'Fairmount', their final home, where the garden was spacious enough for W.G. to maintain a pleasing and English country garden. It was not far from Eltham or the Crystal Palace, and he continued with his club cricket, playing regularly for Eltham. He was quite often seen at the Crystal Palace, which continued as a bustling centre of leisure activities: the FA Cup Final, competed for until then at the Oval, was played there from 1895 to 1914. In 1909 Grace cheered on his home team, Bristol City, in their only Cup Final appearance, but Manchester United, making their first but by no means last Cup Final appearance, were the victors. Sandy Turnbull scored the solitary goal in a rough and not very worthy match from a corner taken by Billy Meredith, almost as legendary a character in the world of football as W. G. Grace in that of cricket. Grace may well have noticed, incidentally, that the Cup Final crowds were now always well over 60,000. Billy Murdoch played club cricket with W.G. who, among other involvements, even kept wicket occasionally for Eltham, spiritedly dealing with the lob-bowling of his son Charles. Murdoch, like Edward Grace, died in 1911. He was 57 and Grace had to bear the stress of Murdoch's death while at his dying brother's bedside. Sadly, Grace had perforce to mark the passing of many fellow-cricketers, and, given his own long playing career, there was always one or another player of his acquaintance growing old and dying. From 1911 only two Grace brothers remained, and it was Alfred, the second eldest, the horse-lover, the only heavy smoker and the one who played least cricket, who lived the longest.

The shadows were lengthening. The beard was quite white. The farewells had to be made. There was the last game. This was in July 1914, for Eltham against Grove Park. In his first game, for West Gloucestershire against Bedminster in July 1857, he had scored 3 not out. Now, in his last innings, symbolically enough, he was again undefeated, on this occasion with 69 to his name. His son, Charles, happily, played beside him that day. Astoundingly, W.G. had thus played in each of 58 consecutive seasons.

There was the last appearance at a first-class match. In June 1914 he went to Lord's for the centenary match, commemorating the hundred years since the initial match, MCC against Hertfordshire, had been played on the third and last Lord's site. A little later that season he visited Lord's for the very last time. The Oval had been commandeered for military purposes, and Jack Hobbs had to take his benefit match across the Thames to Lord's. Grace, that kindly supporter of benefits and testimonials, made this final journey to pay his respects to the comprehensive genius of Jack Hobbs, the finest professional batsman of his, some would argue of any, generation.

There was his last major formal engagement. This was the Lord's Centenary dinner, with Lord Hawke in the chair. C. E. Green spoke movingly of Grace's eminence, and there was a spontaneous standing ovation for him. Grace's loyalty to the MCC had never faltered. 'It has acted', he said in his memoirs, 'with the impartiality of the High Court of Appeal, and has always safeguarded the best interests of the game.' The last benefit match in which W.G. played had been in aid of Philip Need, the dressing-room attendant at Lord's; this was his final practical act of devotion to the club which, year after year, had delighted in advertising that Grace had agreed to take part in all major games.

There was his last public appearance, unsurprisingly a cricket occasion. A match had been organised at Catford Bridge for Whit Monday 1915 in aid of war charities. It had fondly been hoped that the

Champion might play, but he was patently not well enough for that. Nonetheless, he joined in and collected coppers from the crowd for the Belgian refugees who were flooding into a shocked Britain. He was never seen on public show again.

The immediacy of the Great War must have forcibly shaken Grace, that least political of men. The alarums of war had, throughout Grace's life, been indistinct and distant, faintly sounding from South Africa or the Sudan. Now it involved reported atrocities just across the Channel, and the need to succour victimised Belgians through charity cricket matches. Much less horrific but maybe more telling, granted W.G.'s preconceptions, was the presence of the military at the Oval, obliging a Surrey professional to organise his benefit on alien turf. Grace was visibly distressed and disoriented by that clash of nations.

He had one last duty to perform on behalf of cricket and that was help bring it to a shuddering halt. Like most of his generation, W. G. Grace viewed the 1914-18 war in simplistic and moral terms, an unreserved conflict of good against evil. It required total moral and emotional commitment, and, sorrowfully, that other overriding commitment, the one to cricket, had to be sacrificed. What the modern mind has difficulty perhaps in understanding is that it was the seriousness of cricket to its Victorian and Edwardian protagonists which made it a distraction, not its triviality. Rowland Bowen has astutely drawn the distinction between attitudes in the two World Wars in his *Cricket: A History of its Growth and Development throughout the World*. All major and competitive cricket, save for some northern league matches, was stopped in England during World War I, as cricketers turned their full attention to the foe. In World War II efforts were made to provide some good-class cricket by way of diversion for players and entertainment for war-weary spectators. The second war may have been, in the then current adjective, 'total' in its physical involvement, but the 1914-18 war was more 'total' in its psychological engagement.

Archie MacLaren, W.G.'s successor as England's captain, had called youth to the colours in sentiments—'that crowned madman', 'that hog in armour', he called the Kaiser in *World of Cricket*—which sound shamefully jingoistic to modern ears. War had been declared on 4 August 1914 and the British Expeditionary Force, the true 'Old Contemptibles', was soon in action. Barely two weeks later Sir John French, after heavy fighting, was supervising its retreat from Mons. Grace was horror-stricken that cricket could meander on while such events were afoot, and he found it offensive that some cricketers might be dying in the trenches while others cavorted at the wicket. In one of the few direct attempts to publish his own thoughts he ever contemplated, he wrote a letter, not to *The Times* as many would have done, but, as he felt in terms of the readership he sought, more fittingly to the *Sportsman*. It is poignant indeed that his last public act was the tacit acknowledgement, by a man who had eschewed such ideas throughout his life, that politics and sport are inextricably mixed. The letter is dated 27 August 1914:

> There are many cricketers who are already doing their duty but there are many more who do not seem to realise that in all probability they will have to serve either at home or abroad before the war is brought to a conclusion. The fighting on the Continent is very severe and is likely to be prolonged. I think the time has arrived when the county cricket season should be closed, for it is not fitting at a time like this that able-bodied men should be playing day by day, and pleasure-seekers look on. There are so many who are young and able, and are still hanging back. I should like to see all first-class cricketers of suitable age set a good example, and come to the help of their country without delay in its hour of need.

Thus was an important voice added to the recruiting campaign of that hour. The cricket season spluttered and was soon in any case extinguished, and many cricketers, possibly blindly and foolishly, certainly bravely, marched into the darkness of war. Their names, great and small, were to swell the obituary pages of *Wisden* over the next four or five years.

# 13
# A State of Grace

How had cricket reached so far into the consciousness of society that it could be discussed and accepted in the solemn terms of Grace's letter to the *Sportsman*?

W. G. Grace said that cricket 'cultivates the manly attributes'. Church and school encouraged the ideal of cricket as the proving ground. Newbolt's 'There's a deathly hush in the close tonight', with its final stanzas of this remembered in the heat of battle, presaged the dreadful challenge for those who 'played their game in the fields of France'. And, as the Rev. Thomas Waugh wrote in 1894, after death 'The whole redeemed Church of God meets you with the words "Well Played, Sir"!' The games cult arguably altered Christianity. In death, as in life, 'he marks not that you won or lost but how you played the game.'

Cricket was a weighty alternative to, and not a relief from, the war effort: one could not mix business with business, and, for the Christian Englishman, there was no room for both a patriotic war and first-class cricket. It was during Grace's career that cricket had adopted this ritualistic dimension.

In an age of 'games-dominated Tory Imperialism' and when Thomas Carlyle fiercely espoused the notion of the heroic individual, W. G. Grace was the prophetic figure, the Ecce Homo, of Victorian cricket. Each game allowed the ritual Grace personified to unfold, its arcane rigmarole negotiating a slow, Talmudic processional from the pitching to the drawing of stumps, with the white-clad figures (how different, say, from the MCC in 1798 in sky-blue coats, nankeen breeches, hats and green beaver) adding to the trance-like, religious quality. There was even the necromantic rites of the Ashes.

Rowland Bowen wrote of this 'special new aura' with cricket becoming 'somehow a rather saintly game'. He records how W. G. Grace's cousin and Gloucestershire colleague, W. R. Gilbert, had been discovered stealing from his fellow-players. 'The Colonel', as he was nicknamed, had scraped a precarious living mainly as a member of Grace's United South team. When this folded, he turned professional in 1886, but was found pilfering in the sacristy of the dressing room. The matter was kept quiet by the Graces and the culprit, rather in the *Beau Geste* tradition, emigrated to Canada—and nearly ninety years on, Bowen was advised not to publish the story! The sin was too awful to contemplate.

The ceremonial of cricket was respectful. Grace contemptuously dismissed 'barracking' as an Australian coinage, and the Grace brothers were all prepared to deal summarily with barrackers. It was like laughing in church. Even the humour could be church-like. When an MCC side, including Grace, was cheaply dismissed by a public school's opening bowlers, by the names Wood and Stone, the headmaster's scholarly choice of hymn in chapel that evening was 'The heathen in their blindness bow down to Wood and Stone'. The joke is in the dignified tradition of Anglican wit, like 'How should it stand before all resistless Graces?'

Grace also spoke of cricket as marked by 'the absence of occasion for passion', and, while he sometimes honoured this precept in the breach rather than the observance, there is no doubt that W.G. and his fellow Victorians played cricket, as Victorian armies fought such battles as that at Rourke's Drift in 1879, with a strange mixture of bravado and discipline. According to the old professional, when Grace blocked 'em, he blocked 'em for four. In a loop of film of the Champion at practice one notes that Grace adds a potent flourish of his giant's forearms at the moment of execution of every single stroke. It was this passionless enthusiasm, this controlled zeal, which helped Grace and the other maestros of the Golden Age to excel, and thousands of players and spectators approached the sport with the gravity of Phileas Fogg attempting his madcap circumnavigation of the world in eighty days. Ian Peebles has related a story very much in that tradition. Having imperiously plucked the unique talent of Sydney Barnes from nowhere to accompany his touring team to Australia, Archie MacLaren soon discovered that Barnes was cast hard in the William Clarke mould. With their leaky tub in imminent danger of sinking during a storm in the Bay of Biscay, the fearless MacLaren comforted a trembling young amateur: 'Never mind', said MacLaren kindly, 'take consolation from the thought that, if we all drown, Sydney Barnes will drown with us.'

Cricket, therefore, was a discipline, as well as a ritual which became,

in Grace's time, a metaphor for life. In his novel *The Go-Between*, set
in 1900, L. P. Hartley perceptively uses a cricket match between the
country Hall and the village to throw into relief the central plot of Ted
Burgess, small-scale farmer and clandestine lover of Marian
Maudsley, the local magnate's daughter. He is opposed to Lord
Trimingham, stylish crack of the 'Hall' XI and Marian's fiancé.
Young Leo Colston, the go-between of the two lovers, catches out Ted
and wins the game, just as, unavoidably, he leads to the catching out of
the secret affair. 'White clad figures sliding purposefully to and fro . . .
as if a battle were in prospect . . . the ceremony of taking centre . . . its
awful ritual solemnity . . . all our side were in white flannels . . . the
village team . . . distressed me by their nondescript appearance . . . it
was like trained soldiers fighting natives.' Leo's thoughts encapsulate
the mood of the age exquisitely. It was not cricket for Ted Burgess to
enjoy dalliance with Marian, and Ted Burgess shot himself, not for
sinning against Victorian social standards, but, like W. R. Gilbert, for
being discovered.

Then came the 1914-18 war to close that era suddenly and tragically, and with it came the death of W. G. Grace. He died in October
1915. 'Pale death', as *Cricket* had described it in connection with
William Midwinter, visited the Champion on 23 October. He was
some months past his sixty-seventh birthday, and the troops he had
helped recruit were valiantly defending Loos and recuperating from
the savage mauling of Gallipoli.

His health had been poor throughout the year, although he was as
keen as ever on his large Mottingham garden and he had managed to
carry round a collection box at Catford Bridge. His green fingers
never lost their skill. The expertise garnered and the instincts honed
in childhood never deserted him. He could have made a living as a
groundsman as the bowling greens of Crystal Palace and the turf and
plants at 'Fairmount' bore pleasing witness. In the autumn, after the
barren cricket season of 1915 was finished, he had a stroke in his
beloved garden. It was said that this was worsened by the chilling
noise of a Zeppelin raid, and, in fact, the German press were to claim
him as an air-raid casualty, rather as if he was a prize battle-cruiser
which had been torpedoed. H. D. G. Leveson Gower gently teased
him about the Zeppelins, asking how a man who had faced Ernest
Jones and a heavy battery of other fast bowlers could be anxious over
the German airships. 'I could see those beggars,' muttered the dying
man, 'I can't see these.' He made some efforts to rally and rise from
his bed, but to no avail. On 3 November *Punch* said, 'Cricket itself has

suffered the cruellest of wounds since August of last year, and now the Father of it is laid low.'

The layman must see in his death a kind of medical paradox. The iron-clad virility and endurance with which he had, with one lung or two, negotiated his exceedingly energetic life, had led the public and his friends to regard him as, if not immortal, then likely to live long. There was astonishment as well as regret at his passing. Yet, alternately, it could be argued that the very strain he had placed on his constitution over so many years caused it to snap and collapse. His widow, Agnes, who had, very quietly and very undemandingly, succoured hearth and husband over forty-two years, was left, with but two of her four children, and those both faced with the hazards of war, which, fortunately, they survived. Agnes Grace had never sought the limelight, nor had (as she called him) 'the Doctor' where cricket was not the concern. A. A. Thomson has generously reminded us that contemporaries found her 'sweet, gentle, womanly and sympathetic', and that, as a highly competent wife and mother, she 'knew her business, which was nobody else's business, extremely well'. Lord Harris said, simply and fervently, that she was 'a dear'. This quietly efficient and patient lady lived on until March 1930 when, aged 76, she died at Hawkhurst, Kent. *Wisden* said of her that she 'possessed a rare fund of reminiscence of the game', and that 'her memory will be cherished by many cricketers'.

Grace's funeral took place on 26 October, not far from the Crystal Palace and his last home is at Elmers End Cemetery, where both W.G. Junior and Bessie lay buried. Times were difficult, but the funeral was, naturally, very well attended, with a distinctive spread of khaki throughout the assembled mourners. There was widespread grief throughout Britain and the Empire and the news of his death temporarily drove from the newsboys' placards the even more melancholy news of war. He was buried in the family grave, as probably was his wish, but, had the times been peaceful, a more ceremonial occasion would surely have been organised. Although it was but October, the cold struck with a numbing wintriness, adding to the forlornness which hangs over any such sad occasion. Grace's old Gloucestershire comrades, J. A. Bush, wicket-keeper and his best man, R. F. Miles and F. Townsend were in attendance, along with C. E. Green who, months before, had toasted him at the Lord's Centenary dinner, and Philip Need, the last beneficiary of the dozens who had looked not vainly to W.G. for succour. There were both Lord Hawke and Lord Harris, who were to join with Charles Townsend, also present, in

editing the splendid memorial biography of 1919. There was Pelham
Warner, and there was Ranji, the Jam Sahib of Nawanagar, dressed in
the uniform of a staff officer. Some might have hoped for the carriage
of that celebrated son of the west country, back over the Paddington to
Bristol line he had travelled a thousand times, for burial in his native
county. Family wishes and the troubles of war apart, it was fitting
enough that he was buried in London, for it was largely in London
where, both at Lord's and the Oval, he had enjoyed such stirring
exploits and practically created the modern game. It somehow signi-
fied the metropolitan and urban character of cricket.

W.G. has been blessed with devoted and patient biographers. F. S.
Ashley-Cooper, most knowledgeable and understanding of cricket
historians, published *W. G. Grace—Cricketer: A Record of his
Performances in First-Class Matches* in 1916 and the scrupulously
painstaking Mr G. Neville Weston has collated all Grace's cricketing
statistics with meticulous precision. For once in a while, painting by
numbers results in a vivid and breath-taking picture. The broad
brush-strokes are descriptive enough. In first-class cricket, he scored
54,904 runs, took 2,879 wickets, caught 871 and stumped 3. In
minor cricket, he scored 44,936 runs, took 4,446 wickets, caught
641 and stumped 51. In all cricket, he scored 99,840 runs, took
7,325 wickets, caught 1,512 and stumped 54. He was, without
reservation, the Great Cricketer, as Sir Stanley Jackson dubbed him
for the purpose of the Grace Memorial Gates at Lord's. One might
muse of that odd afternoon when it rained, or that other morning
when a dubious lbw decision went against him, as occasions when,
with a mere 140 runs, Grace might so simply have broken into six
figures as a run-getter. One might continue to list the records: the
eight 'double' seasons; the 126 first-class centuries and the 91 in
minor cricket; the fact that he never suffered 'a pair' in first-class
cricket and only four in minor cricket.

One could tease out the statistical proofs endlessly, and they are
important. Grace was as well aware of the significance of ensuring
the ledgers totted up with plenty on the credit side as any Victorian
businessman. It was little wonder that the Victorian so enjoyed the
intricate accountancy of cricket and gloried in its statistical
complexity. The score-book is the counting-house ledger applied to
sport, and the 'double entry' score-sheet allows one to plot the
progress of a game in ball-by-ball detail. The scorers kept the records
with scrupulous care, no Bob Cratchit or Newman Noggs more so.
These were cricket's audited accounts.

Grace's approach to cricket was fundamentally Benthamite. The 'felicific calculus' was a Benthamic phrase which might have been invented especially to describe his batting, not that it was robot-like— Grace was too full of human faults and flavours for that—but because he made it so patently efficient. Put shortly, he concentrated on playing every shot, rather than specialising, as had been the habit when he first began playing, in a certain style; in a famous sentence, 'He turned the old one-stringed instrument into a many-chorded lyre.' This mastered, he deployed that all-round skill with the objective of striking every ball with the appropriate strength and in the most productive direction. He was not aridly mechanical, but extremely functional. This was in the Victorian tradition, but he eschewed what was often its matching trait, that of a fussy ornateness. Grace had all the efficiency, but none of the over-decorative fidgetiness, of the typical item in the Great Exhibition. His batting manner was as sparse, strong and clean as Gregorian plain-chant, and it was highly attractive for that reason. In Ranjitsinhji's telling and cryptic phrase, he 'made utility the criterion of style'.

Prince Ranjitsinhji (albeit ghosted by C. B. Fry) also said that Grace 'revolutionised cricket', turning it from 'an accomplishment into a science'. He was also a social revolutionary, turning cricket finally from a casual players' pastime into a full-scale spectator entertainment. There can be little doubt that his ambiguous social position was one of his assets in the completion of that revolution. Grace could not afford to play cricket year in, year out, complete with a couple of long tours abroad and an insistence on beginning practice in March. He managed to solve this problem without acrimony and without being accused of being the upstart. His talent was his major credential, and his powerful personality helped him carry the day. He was not bred in the amateur tradition of public school and university, but, even more obviously, was not the stuff of which the regular professional was made. The indeterminate position, paradoxically, worked to his advantage. Where in similar circumstances many would have been crushed by receiving the worst of both worlds, Grace was able to seize the best of both. He enjoyed the social perquisites of amateur status, without the anxiety of financial strain, and he left £10,000 when he died, a smallish fortune in 1915. He enjoyed, beyond the dreams of the most well-to-do professional's avarice, the benefits of professionalism, without the social discomforts and occasional humiliations of that position.

Grace was a pragmatist. It was an age which welcomed and

succoured pragmatism in all walks of life. Prior to 1830 it was unlikely he would have managed to sustain such a career; during this century until the last few years, it is unlikely that the powers-that-be would have permitted so overt a demonstration of fortune-hunting. For instance, the habit of newspapers launching testimonials could have openly contravened the amateur ethic and the amateur regulations. Grace was made for so ambivalent an age, and the age was ripe for him. He joined the gallery of engineers, politicians, entrepreneurs and authors who, in the equivocal climate of Victorian England, rose from middling situations to positions of power and influence. Like them, he was a tireless grafter: 'I had to work as hard at cricket as I ever worked at my profession or anything else.'

Grace as well as representing, willy-nilly, all that was characteristic of Victorian and Edwardian cricket, also serves as a reminder that the Victorians were no less commercially-minded than, say, Kerry Packer. If one takes into account his expenses with Gloucestershire, the subsidisation of his general practice by the county, his match fees from the United South of England XI, his captaincy fees with the London County Club (whom he had to sue for his last year's salary in yet another ding-dong row with a board or committee), his healthy spread of testimonials, his ghosted books, articles and the like, and his overseas tours payments, at the most reasonable estimate one must hazard the guess that, between 1870 and 1910, his combined income, direct and indirect, from cricket must have been easily in the region of £120,000. Naturally, he had plentiful outgoings as well, but it means that, by today's valuation, Grace received over the equivalent of a million pounds in the major part of his career. It has been claimed that, by the shaky standards of the day, his rewards were modest and, judged as payments for his worth, they were quite ludicrously small. The point is that he played for the Gentlemen.

Maybe the Victorians were right to gaze with opaque lenses on such blatant eschewal of the amateur ethic, dimly aware that a Nietzschean super-ego, a figure worthy of Carlyle's resonant tributes, was at work, lifting their sub-culture from the ruck of the present and handing it on to the future. What a mixture of cant and sentiment the Victorians could stomach! They must have believed it all implicitly, and set at nothing that which was not in honour of their country and their creed. Grace was, after all, in another *Punch* compliment, 'unmatched, unchallengeable best'.

Grace was the sort of man whose obituaries begin with apologies such as 'whatever his other foibles'. Super-ego as cricketer he certainly was—'the great Englishman playing the great English game in English fields', as Norman Birkett splendidly wrote—but, as a man, he was the same mortal mix of efficiencies and deficiencies as any of us. In fairness, his unpleasant characteristics were not unusual in Victorians and may look the worse for being peered at through modern eyes. He was dictatorial, at times sharp-tempered and over-suspicious of slights. As a parent, one might guess that he was some-what overbearing, and, as a husband, not unvaryingly considerate, which is to say he was a normal Victorian family man. That he led a full and boisterous life cannot be gainsaid and, given that his several friends admired him genuinely and that his kindnesses were manifold throughout that crowded life, the balance of good with ill was more than maintained. He was regarded with as sincere affection at a distance by thousands of enthusiasts among the British and Australian publics as at close hand by family, colleagues and patients.

It is when one examines Grace as a sportsman that the portrait darkens a shade. It is difficult now to distinguish the gospel from the apocrypha in the testament of anecdotes told over and again about his artfulness. However, it is significant that these are the tales, true or embellished, that are related, and not stories which pay tribute to his docility or his chivalry. In a sense the truth is what was believed and what was handed down. The smoke may be not only more visible but also more interesting than the fire.

It is said that he did not break the rules, but that, through a canny knowledge of them, he was often able to procure his own ends without deliberate cheating. The old professional, asked by Neville Cardus whether Grace acted illegally, said wryly that he was too clever for that. The laws of cricket are indeed flexible, and, if not used as guidelines and with an accompanying spirit of goodwill, they provide rich pickings for a sea lawyer such as Grace. He adhered tightly to the laws, however trivial or artificial the incident, and he could be exceedingly hard on umpires. His louring presence, with either his belligerent demand for a wicket or his incredulous disgust at so audacious an appeal against him, must have made it hard labour for ex-professionals, trying to eke out a meagre living and desperately reliant on the good offices of the likes of Grace. Even allowing for the fact that umpiring standards were, at some levels and in some places, neither high nor impartial, his attempts practically to instruct umpires in their duties bordered on the unfair and the autocratic. His occasional habit of appealing successfully and then confessing to the victim trailing back to the pavilion that he had not actually been 'out' is another case of the letter rather than the spirit of the law being obeyed. Gilbert Jessop has described how MacLaren hit his wicket in a county match, but it was adjudged as being after the completion of the shot by the umpire William Shrewsbury, brother to Grace's favourite batsman, Arthur. MacLaren went on to score 96 not out. 'W.G. was inconsolable for the rest of the game' wrote Jessop, 'and nothing would induce him to believe in the correctness of the decision. It was obvious to many of us that no injustice had been done, but I'm afraid few of us had the pluck to voice our opinions to that effect.' Alfred Lyttelton was vastly amused, after dismissing Grace for the second time cheaply for Middlesex, to note 'the ominous look on the usually genial face'. As he returned to the dressing-tent, there occurred 'the simultaneous departure of the Gloucestershire team from the back of the tent to avoid facing the explosion.' Batting or fielding, his dogmatism and fury were powerful forces. 'Pavilion, you', he would, with a dramatic pointing gesture, dismiss a batsman who showed some signs of argument. Yet, when one of his favourites was given out at the Oval, he stormed from the balcony: 'Shan't have it; can't have  · it; and I won't have it.' In 1912 the *Sportsman* magazine commented on 'The weakness of W.G. for dwelling at the wicket after the umpire's decision.' The writer quoted the match against XXII of Birmingham in 1874, when, his score on 56, the mid-off appeared to miss the ball but had momentarily lost it between arm and body. Recovering, he easily ran out the misled Grace, who gave 'a look of disapproval and was about to speak out'. The Yorkshire umpire, Webster, fearlessly thwarted him: 'If you had been Jesus Christ I should have given you out.'

He talked incessantly on the field and this could be extremely off-putting, especially so when the loquacious Edward was situated on the opposite side of the wicket. Then the cross-talk reached music-hall proportions, and, on one occasion, as aristocratic a gentleman as Lord Hawke felt obliged to scold them. As well as continuous chatter as a weapon in the cricketing war, Grace was not beyond shouting 'Miss it!' when a fielder was about to catch him out, which, by any stand-ards, lacks refinement. Among his rumoured stratagems was the busi-ness of inviting innocent batsmen to gaze toward the sun at a passing flight of birds in the hope of affecting their eye-sight adversely, and (presumably lacking the magical eyesight of his elder brother Edward) shouting 'Woman!' at the toss, and claiming either Britannia or Victoria as his selection.

Sometimes the tactics were quite involved. The brothers, during a club match, arranged for a telegram to be sent to the ground, pretending to call Henry, then rather longer in the tooth, to a mythical patient. The agile Jack Board was then recruited as a sprightly substitute. It all seems rather unnecessary for players of such ability to stoop to such silly pranks. Maybe it is a prudish and puritanical attitude, and cricket should never be a humourless game, but many of these efforts were clumsy and unfunny, even by the heavy-handed standards of Victorian comedy.

Bernard Darwin, in part apology, has explained that 'the less serious the match, the greater the licence of humour'. Naturally enough, Grace could hardly have been expected to take a minor club match quite as gravely as a Test match, although, in truth, he normally did while batting. The point is that the other players, the victims of Grace's ponderous antics, were probably trying, at their own level, to take the game seriously. When Grace was a boy, earnestly attempting to prove himself as a youthful club cricketer, he would have probably found it untoward and disconcerting to find some huge opponent, talking loudly, bullying umpires, practising barrack-room law, and indulging in strategic buffoonery. Of course it is easier, at this distance of time, to grin at cricket's artful dodger, and probably at the time, because he was a famed and respected figure, his inferiors felt obliged to give an impression of enjoyment. Often they must, in reality, have felt that E. W. Swanton's verdict—that Grace had 'a tinge of genial rascality'—errs somewhat on the side of charity.

To make matters worse, he was not too keen on the lèse-majesté of a joke against himself. He could enjoy children and non-cricketing gags. He chuckled heartily over the child who asked him a second time in an hour for his autograph. When reminded of the prior occasion, the young collector explained that he had swapped W. G. Grace's for 'Dan Leno's and a couple of bishops'. But when cricket was in progress, Grace could be offended. Once, when playing against Kortright, the Essex fast bowler, Grace entered into lively controversy over what he forthrightly maintained was a bump-ball caught and bowled by Walter Mead. Soon afterwards the fiery Kortright removed two of Grace's stumps, and, as the doctor strode toward the dressing room, the satisfied bowler became the first recorded spokesman of a clinching line since associated with every fast bowler in the business. 'What, are you going, Doctor?', asked Kortright. 'There's still one standing.' Grace was deeply wounded. He went so far as to say that he had never been so insulted in all his life.

He did not relish hecklers. There was the match after the one at

Grimsby when, with his second son's birth to celebrate part-way through, he had scored 400—although many Grimsby folk claimed that it was only 399 and that W.G. asked an obliging scorer to round up the sum. The next game was against the stiffer opposition of the United North at Huddersfield, and Grace managed but 5 runs. As he dolefully returned to the pavilion, a stentorian Yorkist voice pointed out that, on this occasion, he was not playing against 'a lot of cockle-'awkers'. Grace did not relish the gibe at all.

Yet he could be patently kind. A rather backward and stuttering Gloucester youth called Ernest was the butt of his fellows, who cruelly hoaxed him with a forged note inviting him to play for the county. He turned up on the morning of the match and W.G. was compassion itself. When he realised the trick, he gently told the stammering Ernest that perhaps he would not be required for the actual match, but would he bowl to W.G. in the nets? This he energetically did, and, as a final act of charity, he allowed Ernest the pleasure of bowling him.

On occasion he would slyly change fielders—a silent transference from first slip to short-leg, for instance—with the bowler in mid-run, in order perhaps to engineer a catch. And he was much too crafty to be caught in his own trap. When facing Briggs of Lancashire at Bristol once, A. N. Hornby tried such a stratagem, but, even as Briggs was completing his run-in, W.G. was crying out 'I can see what you're doing.'

Apart from the considerable strain on Grace to repeat and sustain his success, another motivation for his sometimes extraordinary conduct was perhaps his boyishness, using that word not in its everyday connotation as a sort of spirited skittishness, but, in dictionary terms, as 'of, or proper to, a boy'. Grace's modern biographers have shrewdly commented on this abiding trait in his character.

Clifford Bax said bluntly 'He was a case of arrested development and remained, intellectually, always at the age of sixteen.' A. A. Thomson writes of him being 'very boylike', while never shirking the responsibilities of adult life, and Darwin said 'He had all the schoolboy's love for elementary and boisterous jokes, his distaste for learning, his desperate and undisguised keenness; his guilelessness and his guile; his occasional pettishness and pettiness; his endless power of recovering his good spirits.'

Perhaps this assessment is the most discerning ever registered about W.G. To the modern mind and eye he appears as very like an exaggeratedly over-grown schoolboy. It was, of course, a conventional type of schoolboy, the prototype for Frank Richards's Greyfriars alumni, like Harry Wharton and Bob Cherry, or Talbot Baines Reed's fourth form at St Dominics. Tom Brown and Stalky and Co. had earlier set the tradition in train. Like them, Grace was no academic, for, books on whist apart, he rarely read let alone wrote anything. Like them he had soundness of sense and steadiness of judgement, what the Duke of Wellington had called horse-sense. Like them, he enjoyed hearty and wholesome friendships, and was diffident, even suspicious of too much formal politeness. Like them, his occasional spats of anger and frustration quickly gave way to more optimistic and genial moods. And, in his memoirs, Grace was to make unnecessary and misleading play of his own so-called time at 'boarding school'.

Those literary caricatures represented the noble side of schoolboy-hood. Grace was no two-dimensional cardboard model, so he also exhibited the ignoble side. Certainly he energetically espoused the jolly wheeze or jape, but oftentimes, as in the playground of reality, it was a little malicious and insensitive. Perhaps Harry Wharton's cheerful jokes at Billy Bunter's expense are not, on profounder con-sideration, all that pleasant. Amusingly, Grace was apparently guilty of the classic schoolboy sin of cowardice in the face of soap and water. It has been written that, like Samuel Johnson, he had 'no passion for clean linen', and he certainly found A. N. Hornby's affection for cold baths nothing less than a perverse aberration. 'Ugh, Monkey', he snorted at Hornby as he indulged in his chilly douche, 'you make me shudder.' It was the view of Viscount Cobham that Grace's was 'one of the dirtiest necks I ever kept wicket behind'.

If Grace was so neglectful of his personal hygiene and laundry, and given the fibre and heaviness of his old fashioned clothing, then he must have grown decidedly grubby during a long, sweaty innings or bustling bowling spell. It may seem an odd trait in a medical practi-tioner, for, although the germ theory was still in its infancy as Grace's medical career was closing, the connection between dirt and disease was already recognised. But it would appear that Grace was a resourceful, unsentimental but kindly doctor, not much given to extravagant theorising. One remembers his summary emergency treatment of Croome and Fox on the cricket field. There is a boy-scout flavour about his methods: they were as brisk and uncomplicated as the sanest patrol leader's.

However, the major factor in Grace's 'boyish-ness' was undoubt-edly his obsession with sport. Without inferring that he had little time or thought for his family or his profession, the fact is that cricket, and in any spare time a range of other games, dominated his life. His eagerness to play cricket, from practice in the shivery days of later winter through to matches on the darkening evenings of autumn, was legendary. From infancy beyond what now would be retiring age, he played and played day after day, at every level from village green to the Test arena. He hogged the batting, and detested being out. Until very late in his career he was equally determined to monopolise the bowling. His contemporary, C. E. Green, describing him as 'a real glutton for cricket', tells how Grace, when approached by I. D. Walker, the captain of the Gentlemen of the South, about a change from his bowling, advised, 'I tell you what, I'll go on at the other end.' This childlike greed for cricket goes far toward explaining that equally childlike testiness, slyness and skullduggery which he so often displayed in his avid appetite for runs and wickets.

He died as the lights were going out all over Europe; and, in his passing, he seemed to symbolise the closure of an era. One might be forgiven for the conjecture that it was. Perhaps it was more than a dismally neat coincidence. When old Martha Grace died, the game between Lancashire and Gloucestershire at Old Trafford was abandoned, and, when Edward Grace died, the flags at Northampton, where Gloucester were the visitors, were immediately flown at half-mast. When William Gilbert Grace died cricket had already been abandoned and the flags lowered. He died in the autumn following the first season in which no first-class cricket had been played in England since the very concept of such cricket had been specified. Grace, with his juvenile refusal to take politics seriously, was bewildered by the war; he hated, and rightly, the thought of cricketers and other young men being 'mown down', but, more than that, he was bewildered and, for all his full-hearted courage, frightened by it. But for Grace the immediate, searing wound was the total collapse and absence of cricket. Into that hollowness must have drained the remnants of the Champion's resolve to live. His obsession starved, his will was vanquished.

Thus the salient element in Grace's make-up was probably a defiant reluctance to grow into maturity, a determination well disguised by his colossal physical powers and feats. He was, so to speak, a goblin in giant's clothing. Perhaps the lesson, dinned Jesuitically into his unmoulded mind before he started school, that cricket was to be his forte, did take an unyielding hold and become his lifetime's credo and driving-force. His over-anxious proxy reincarnation in W.G. Junior underlines the point, as possibly does some of his not always sensible espousal of gilded young public-school boys and university students at the expense of professionals and club cricketers. The *Manchester Guardian* criticised W.G.'s reminiscences for their grudging reference, for example, to Richard Barlow. 'He dismisses the famous Lancashire professional with a shorter notice than he bestows upon that illustrious cricketer Prince Christian Victor of Schleswig-Holstein', was the *Guardian*'s sardonic and loyalist comment. Barlow, who did after all dismiss Grace no less than thirty-one times, was described by the maestro, or at least by his ghost writer, as 'monotony incarnate'.

Contemporaries saw him as immature. Arthur Porritt wrote: 'About Dr W. G. Grace there was something indefinable—like the simple faith of a child—which arrested and fascinated me. He was a big grown-up boy, just what a man who only lived when he was in the open air might be expected to be.' An old friend of W.G. told Bernard Darwin that Grace was 'just a great big schoolboy in everything he did', while Colonel Philip Trevor, who knew Grace passing well, said he was 'a great big baby', although, in tones more maternal than martial, he added his opinion that most men often were. It is also true that, as far as Grace was concerned, a boy's best friend is his mother. It is unlikely that any woman, not even his wife or his adored daughter, Bessie, quite replaced that dominant lady in his affections. The only zephyr rustle to disturb the seeming calm of W.G.'s maternal and marital relations is a peculiar jotting inserted in the Lord's library copy of his reminiscences. The slip of newsprint quotes Claire's saw: 'Woe to the man who trusts his heart to a woman, changeful as the breeze.' Then there is Grace's curt addition: 'I can testify to this truth.' Whether this refers to some early (or late) affection, or to any change in his wife's feelings, or, which is not unlikely, it is the jocular rejoinder of the bluff Victorian male, one cannot be sure. What is certain is that he was not referring to his mother, whose death wounded him dreadfully. His tutor and brother-in-law, the Rev. J. W. Dann, who married Grace's sister, Blanche, has stressed W.G.'s 'wonderful love and admiration for his mother'. Like many another man some way retarded towards boyhood, the maternal link formed probably the strongest liaison of his emotional life.

This did not, of course, amount to any sort of derangement. In many respects Grace led an extremely stable and well-rounded life, and, for instance, his eagerness to see his son succeed or his affection for spoofs, or indeed his devotion to his mother, is no proof of abnormality. But Grace's junior-school mentality did inform and slant his approach to life, giving it if not its exclusive then its most persistent dimension. Furthermore, one would hesitate to press an interpretation even to such modified lengths were it not that his generation and his era were characterised by a similar adherence to boyhood.

In 1904 J. M. Barrie's *Peter Pan* was first produced. Baden-Powell published *Scouting for Boys* in 1908. These were, in their very separate ways, the standard texts of the denial of growing up. In the 1914-18 war, the adventures of Lawrence of Arabia, part genuine, part fantasy, exposed both the brilliant virtues and the depressing vices of sustained immaturity. His apparently asexual temperament and overheatedly imaginative mind typified that gifted adult, emotionally stunted about or before adolescence, who recurs throughout late Victorian and Edwardian life. F. Anstey's novel *Vice Versa* took a burlesque view of this proclivity. The Bultitudes, father and son, find themselves magically exchanged with a resultant compound of apprehensions on both sides.

So, if Grace was to any degree fixated in boyhood, he was in good company. Many of those around him, having been schooled in something like the same habits, would notice nothing of radical distortion, and it is perhaps significant that several of them did actually comment on this tendency in Grace. Even they noted the trait, but, in noting it, they generally admired it. Some commentators have pointed out that the very British affection for games is child-like. Was this—does it remain—a Peter Pan syndrome? That refusal to grow up has been blamed on the insularity of these islands and on the introverted and secluded education of its higher echelons, as well as on the strict convention of Victorian domesticity. It was only late in the century, and more especially after the publication of Lewis Carroll's *Alice in Wonderland* in 1865, that the mood shifted and the child was not so literally viewed and treated as father to the man. The denial of the proper development of childhood may have assisted in the devotion felt by adults for a child-like pursuit, as they unconsciously filled the emotional and psychological vacuum left. Possibly men like Grace, who had adult responsibilities and values thrust upon them in childhood, and who played, literally or metaphorically, with grown-ups at nine, spent some of the rest of their lives catching up the missing stages of child development.

Be that as it may, cricket itself came to a fulsome maturity under the Victorians with W. G. Grace, both at home and, under the British flag, abroad. In the last decade of the last century and in the first decade of this, cricket ripened to its proudest flower, and is unlikely ever to bloom so again. It was a Victorian triumph, reaching its zenith late in that era and maintaining its glory throughout the Edwardian period, that apposite epilogue to Victorianism. Brilliant although the quality of play was in this period, it was also in its cultural and social aspects that cricket reached its highest points of development. The two—the expertise of the players and cricket's socio-cultural context—naturally interlocked. Part of, for instance, cricket's tremendous popularity at that time stemmed from the unparalleled zest and command of its exponents, while, in turn, they were doubtless inspired by being revered as the high priests of an almost sacred cult. Certainly all the lines of cricketing development peaked together to create a well-rounded and complete social phenomenon. If cricket had demonstrated that the English never grew up but indulged, in all classes, in child-like pastime, then 1914 was a national coming of age. W.G. himself sounded the clarion, and told young men to beat their cricket bats into rifles and turn their attention from Australia to Germany.

Arguably, cricket and Grace died together. Naturally, this does not mean that cricket, as a sport, was played no more. A clearer statement is that cricket atrophied then and has not, in any major way, evolved further since that time. The game had completed its development and was practised at its highest degree of competence. All-round fielding and field placing may now be more generally efficient and consistently so, but the actual skills of fielding, as well as those of batting, bowling and wicket-keeping, have not basically changed, and, although equalled, have not, in chief, been bettered. That imagined transferability of players, from age to age, so beloved of the buffs of any sport, is not as difficult in cricket as in other sports: compare, for instance, the Wimbledon tennis championships with those of a hundred years ago or even less.

An illuminating example is that cricket (like football in earlier times) has no fouls or sanctions: a typically Victorian stance on the cult of sportsmanship and acceptance of the law. A cricket match cannot progress far without the players' self-discipline and without their basic acceptance of the overall structure of the game. If players actively started to 'foul' one another, umpires would have little chance to arbitrate and no penalties to award. One should not whitewash cricket. There is and has been plenty of sharp practice of the Grace brand, ranging from appropriately prepared pitches to rank psychological warfare; but it has not yet had to accept the late twentieth-century stock-in-trade of the 'professional foul'.

The fact is that, for better or worse, cricket is a Victorian game, and represents the vices and virtues of that stimulating and arrogant epoch. What we have played, watched and read about since 1919 has been the celebration of that ritual, and, particularly in the inter-war years, it was blessed with writers worthy of that reverential treatment: the mellifluous prose of Neville Cardus helped enshrine cricket in this manner. It was he who made the point eloquently apropos W. G. Grace: 'easily the most spectacular man that ever played the game'. Cardus continued, 'He was the Dr Johnson of cricket—as full of his subject, as kindly and as irascible, and just as dogmatic in his dispensations of authority.'

This ability to watch cricket, backwards and from memory, means that its escapist quality is finely marked. It is a reverie, and, in one sense, it is anticlimatic. It has been a cultural effort to make time stand still and re-live, over and over, through the gifts of generations of cricketers, that Victorian experience. The continuous re-catching of that mood has implied a maintenance of the studied manners as well as the peculiar skills of the game, despite internal fiddling with the small points on the laws and alterations to the county competitions.

There are many who watch this processional of first-class cricket in a numbed state of ambivalence. On the one hand, they will wax sardonic about the snobbery and fuddy-duddyness of the MCC; on the other hand, they will be as shaken and offended as the blimpiest greybeard on his high chair in the Long Room at Lord's at the sight of a white sun hat, never mind a protective helmet. The impact of Kerry Packer was largely cultural and psychological. It was the threat to the context of the game rather than to the quality of the performance which most offended his opponents and led them into legal byways. The shock that players would prefer to earn more money in trumped-up exhibition matches in the strangest of conditions and with no hope of them being designated 'first class' was acute. Many of the Packer fancies— coloured uniforms, white balls, night matches—are much less revolutionary than the changes cricket underwent in the nineteenth century. But by the Edwardian era the cricket authorities had more or less decided that all was well in the best of all possible worlds, and that a self-perpetuating oligarchy could nurse cricket, petrified at that point in time, for ever. It has meant that cricket's twentieth-century organisers have out-Heroded Herod. They have been considerably more conservationist and conservative than their predecessors, precisely because their referential frame was in the past—and that of their predecessors had been in the future.

That cricket since 1919 has been little more than a breath-taking and gripping exercise in mellow nostalgia and romantic anticlimax is a brave claim. But, even if it is an unfair hypothesis, it is undeniable that by those twenty or thirty years before 'the great game' of 1914, cricket had reached its highest and headiest point ever. It reigned in triumph as the premier game of England and her Empire in years when England and her Empire commanded the world's attention, if not always affection. And at the helm throughout this period was W. G. Grace. The then editor of *Wisden*, Sydney Pardon, said in the obituary in the 1916 edition: 'when he was in his prime no sun was too hot and no day too long for him', and, from a million incidents, he perceptively chose as the epitome of Grace his innings of 221 against Middlesex at Clifton in 1885, during which he stayed at the bedside of a patient the whole night.

Grace, in large part, created modern cricket and established it as a social and cultural reflection of his age. In at least two ways—the well-paid gentleman and the schoolboy in ogre's guise—he appears superficially paradoxical, but, in depth, this was all of a piece with his Victorian surrounds. An interesting final test of both his consummate greatness as a cricketer and the curious petrifaction of cricket in its Victorian-English stage of evolution is to wonder whether W. G. Grace would be an automatic choice for England's all-time cricket team.

The answer must be a resounding and unqualified 'Yes', and it is the essence of the point that, for any Victorian jockeys, boxers, footballers, athletes, swimmers and tennis-players, it would be difficult to make a similar case. If a benign providence could reincarnate the Champion, his eyes would glint at the sight of the bland, docile wickets and well-manicured outfields, and, given the news that boundaries were reduced to a shorter yardage, he might give vent to one of his high-pitched chuckles. His quick cricket intelligence—what *Punch* called his 'Ulysses-like astuteness of tactics'—would briskly assimilate the latest vagaries of the no ball and lbw rules, and he would be pleased to learn that, at all levels, only eleven fielders would be mustered to foil his efforts. He would sniff appreciatively at the improvement in equipment, while probably declining the use of the helmet. He would be gratified to note that, in each team, more fielders reached the standard set by himself, in his prime, and by his brothers, by Gilbert Jessop, by Hirst, Braund, MacLaren and others, than in his own age. And his superb powers of sighting, hitting and placing deliveries would, to his enjoyment, be rather more challenged than of yore by more versatile field-setting. In short, he would probably soon feel acclimatised and prepared to take his place in any first-class side and, as supreme batsman and devastating all-rounder, perform with distinction in every present-day style of encounter from a forty-overs thrash to the solemnities of the five- or six-day Test. After all, it is, more or less, his game: in the words of E. V. Lucas, in Grace's obituary in *Punch*, 'There will never be another not only to play cricket as Grace did, but to be cricket as Grace was.'

D. L. A. Jephson's valedictory verse ended:

> Dead; and from death a myriad memories rise
> Deathless; we thank you, friend, that once you lived.

# Bibliographical Note and Author's Acknowledgements

Eleven words is the total of my technical conversation so far with a first-class cricketer. The school were playing their local rivals at Old Trafford and were two down for no runs. Venturing forth to stop the rot, I found myself addressed at the pavilion gate by the redoubtable Harry Makepeace. 'For Christ's sake', he growled, 'put a bit of wood to it, lad.' The story of my match-winning fifteen (our opponents having collapsed for 43) must be told elsewhere: the point is that I lay no claim to cricketing know-how and, for the purposes of this book, I have pillaged cricket's literature as ruthlessly as W.G. slaughtered attack after attack. By way of thankful and sincere acknowledgement, and as a guide to further reading, I list the chief works which I have found most valuable, concentrating here on the cricket books and making no mention of the dozens of general books on the Victorian period which have also been extremely helpful.

Two histories of cricket must first be acknowledged. There is the comprehensive and scholarly *A History of Cricket. Volume One: From the Beginnings to the First World War* (1962 edition) by H. S. Altham, and there is the spikily controversial and vigorously wide-ranging *Cricket: A History of its Growth and Development throughout the World* (1970) by Rowland Bowen. Together they form an indispensable base for a study such as this. Cricket is fortunate in that its historians are elegant stylists, and vice versa. Thus Neville Cardus and John Arlott automatically enter any such bibliographical note, for both of them provide historical insights and literary pleasures in abundance. From the extensive Cardus canon, I would pick his *English Cricket* (1945), a brilliant dissection of the game, including Grace's role in its development; while in *Arlott and Trueman on Cricket* (1977) John Arlott traced the evolution of cricket with relish and realism, in particular with his persuasive chapter 'The Price of Grace'. Two others have attempted to set cricket in its socio-economic context. *Beyond the Boundary* (1963) by C. L. R. James is a most penetrating and highly readable analysis, and his tempered judgement of Grace has not been bettered. *English Cricket* (1978) by Christopher Brookes is yet another well-researched, intelligent and clear-eyed appraisal.

Then there are the several excellent biographies of W. G. Grace, each offering the reader special and varying details and conjectures, all of them compiled with dedication. W. Methven-Brownlee's *W. G. Grace* (1887);

F. S. Ashley-Cooper's *W. G. Grace—Cricketer: A Record of his Performances in First-Class Matches* (1916); and Lord Hawke, Lord Harris and Sir Home Gordon, *W. G. Grace, The Memorial Biography* (1919) were the most solid early achievements. More recently, there have been two delightful biographies: Bernard Darwin's *W. G. Grace* (1934) and A. A. Thomson's *The Great Cricketer* (1957), both full of pleasantly modulated description and good-humoured assessment. For my own purposes, I owe a considerable debt to A. G. Powell and S. Canynge Caple and their book *The Graces* (1948) and to Grahame W. Parker for his painstaking and fascinating account of my ancestor's career in his 'The Midwinter File' (*Wisden*, 1971).

I have been able to study other aspects of Grace's life and times in the Lord's library, during which I have much appreciated the courteous, expert guidance of the curator, Stephen Green. I have also benefited substantially in all of this from the sagacious counsels and kindly encouragement of my publisher, John Bright-Holmes.

I can only hope that this attempt to take stock of W. G. Grace and to place him historically in his regional, national and imperial setting does some justice to the perceptive and excellent authors acknowledged here.

# Index

This is an index of persons mentioned in the text with, where necessary, a brief phrase by way of description.